Five Dialogues

PLATO

Five Dialogues

Second Edition

Euthyphro
Apology
Crito
Meno
Phaedo

Translated by
G. M. A. GRUBE

Revised by
JOHN M. COOPER

Hackett Publishing Company, Inc.
Indianapolis/Cambridge

Copyright © 2002 by Hackett Publishing Company, Inc.

14 13 12 11 10   6 7 8 9 10 11

For further information, please address:
  Hackett Publishing Company, Inc.
  P.O. Box 44937
  Indianapolis, IN 46244-0937
  www.hackettpublishing.com

Cover design by Listenberger & Associates

Library of Congress Cataloging-in-Publication Data
Plato.
    [Dialogues. English. Selections]
    Five Dialogues / Plato ; translated by G.M.A. Grube. — 2nd ed. / revised
by John M. Cooper.
        p.   cm.
    Includes bibliographical references.
    Contents: Euthyphro—Apology—Crito—Meno—Phaedo.
    ISBN 0-87220-633-5 (pbk.)—ISBN 0-87220-634-3 (cloth)
    1. Philosophy, Ancient.   I. Grube, G.M.A. (George Maximilian
Anthony)   II. Title.
B358.G7813   2002
184—dc21   2002022754

ISBN-13: 978-0-87220-634-2 (cloth)
ISBN-13: 978-0-87220-633-5 (pbk.)

CONTENTS

Preface to the Second Edition   vii

Introduction   ix

Euthyphro   1

Apology   21

Crito   45

Meno   58

Phaedo   93

Suggestions for Further Reading   155

PREFACE TO THE SECOND EDITION

The translations of Plato's *Euthyphro, Apology, Crito, Meno,* and *Phaedo* presented here are taken from Hackett Publishing Company's epoch-making Plato, *Complete Works* (third printing, 2001), prepared under my editorship. In the revised form in which George Grube's distinguished translations appear here, they present Plato's wonderfully vivid and moving—as well as challenging—portrayal of Socrates, and of the philosophic life, in clear, contemporary, down-to-earth English that nonetheless preserves and accurately conveys the nuances of Plato's and Socrates' philosophical ideas. For this new edition I have added a number of new footnotes explaining various places and events in Athens, features of Greek mythology, and the like, to which Socrates and his interlocutors make reference. At a number of places I have introduced further revisions in the translations.

John M. Cooper

INTRODUCTION

At the time of his trial and execution in 399 B.C., Socrates was seventy years of age. He had lived through the Periclean age when Athens was at the pinnacle of her imperial power and her cultural ascendancy, then through twenty-five years of war with Sparta and the final defeat of Athens in 404, the oligarchic revolution that followed, and, finally, the restoration of democracy. For most of this time he was a well-known character, expounding his philosophy of life in the streets of Athens to anyone who cared to listen. His "mission," which he explains in the *Apology*, was to expose the ignorance of those who thought themselves wise and to try to convince his fellow citizens that every man is responsible for his own moral attitudes. The early dialogues of Plato, of which *Euthyphro* is a good example, show him seeking to define ethical terms and asking awkward questions. There is no reason to suppose that these questions were restricted to the life of the individual. Indeed, if he questioned the basic principles of democracy and adopted towards it anything like the attitude Plato attributes to him, it is no wonder that the restored democracy should consider him to have a bad influence on the young.

With the development of democracy and in the intellectual ferment of the fifth century, a need was felt for higher education. To satisfy it, there arose a number of traveling teachers who were called the Sophists. All of them taught rhetoric, the art of public speaking, which was a powerful weapon, since all the important decisions were made by the assemblies of adult male citizens or in the courts with very large juries. It is not surprising that Socrates was often confused with these Sophists in the public mind, for both of them were apt to question established and inherited values. But their differences were vital: the Sophists professed to put men on the road to success, whereas Socrates disclaimed that he taught anything; his conversations aimed at discovering the truth, at acquiring that knowledge and understanding of life and its values that he thought were the very basis of the good life and of philosophy, to him a moral as well as an intellectual pursuit. Hence his celebrated paradox that virtue is knowledge and that when men do wrong, it is only because they do not *know* any better. We are often told that in this theory Socrates ignored the will, but that is in part a misconception. The aim is not to choose the right but to become the sort of person who *cannot* choose the wrong and who no longer has any choice in the matter. This is what he sometimes expresses as becoming like a god, for the gods, as he puts it in *Euthyphro* (10d), love the pious (and so, the right) because it is right; they cannot do otherwise and no longer have any choice at all, and they cannot be the cause of evil.

The translations in this volume give the full Platonic account of the drama of Socrates' trial and death and provide vivid presentations of Socrates' discussions with his friends and younger contemporaries on the nature of piety, the justice of obedience to state authority, the relation between philosophical knowledge and human virtue, and the wonders, as well as the demands, of the life devoted to philosophy. The references to the coming trial and its charges in *Euthyphro* are a kind of introduction to this drama. The *Apology* is Plato's version of Socrates' speech to the jury in his own defense. In *Crito* we find Socrates refusing to save his life by escaping into exile. *Meno* shows Socrates debating in his characteristic way with Meno on the nature and teachability of human virtue (goodness), and also examining Meno's slave-boy on a question of geometry, in order to prove the preexistence of our souls and our ability to learn ("recollect") truths by rigorously examining our own opinions. *Phaedo* gives an account of his discussion with his friends in prison on the last day of his life, mostly on the question of the immortality of the soul.

The influence of Socrates on his contemporaries can hardly be exaggerated, especially on Plato but not on Plato alone, for a number of authors wrote on Socrates in the early fourth century B.C. And his influence on later philosophers, largely through Plato, was also very great. This impact, on his contemporaries at least, was due not only to his theories but in large measure to his character and personality, that serenely self-confident personality that emerges so vividly from Plato's writings, and in particular from his account of Socrates' trial, imprisonment, and execution.

NOTE: *With few exceptions, this translation follows Burnet's Oxford text.*

G. M. A. Grube

EUTHYPHRO

Euthyphro is surprised to meet Socrates near the king-archon's court, for Socrates is not the kind of man to have business with courts of justice. Socrates explains that he is under indictment by one Meletus for corrupting the young and for not believing in the gods in whom the city believes. After a brief discussion of this, Socrates inquires about Euthyphro's business at court and is told that he is prosecuting his own father for the murder of a laborer who is himself a murderer. His family and friends believe his course of action to be impious, but Euthyphro explains that in this they are mistaken and reveal their ignorance of the nature of piety. This naturally leads Socrates to ask, What is piety? And the rest of the dialogue is devoted to a search for a definition of piety, illustrating the Socratic search for universal definitions of ethical terms, to which a number of early Platonic dialogues are devoted. As usual, no definition is found that satisfies Socrates.

The Greek term hosion *means, in the first instance, the knowledge of the proper ritual in prayer and sacrifice and of course its performance (as Euthyphro himself defines it in 14b). But obviously Euthyphro uses it in the much wider sense of pious conduct generally (e.g., his own), and in that sense the word is practically equivalent to righteousness (the justice of the* Republic), *the transition being by way of conduct pleasing to the gods.*

Besides being an excellent example of the early, so-called Socratic dialogues, Euthyphro *contains several passages with important philosophical implications. These include those in which Socrates speaks of the one Form, presented by all the actions that we call pious (5d), as well as the one in which we are told that the gods love what is pious because it is pious; it is not pious because the gods love it (10d). Another passage clarifies the difference between genus and species (11e–12d).*

G.M.A.G.

2   EUTHYPHRO:[1] What's new, Socrates, to make you leave your usual
haunts in the Lyceum and spend your time here by the king-archon's
court?[2] Surely you are not prosecuting anyone before the king-archon
as I am?

SOCRATES: The Athenians do not call this a prosecution but an
indictment, Euthyphro.

b   EUTHYPHRO: What is this you say? Someone must have indicted you,
for you are not going to tell me that you have indicted someone else.

SOCRATES: No indeed.

EUTHYPHRO: But someone else has indicted you?

SOCRATES: Quite so.

EUTHYPHRO: Who is he?

SOCRATES: I do not really know him myself, Euthyphro. He is apparently young and unknown. They call him Meletus, I believe. He belongs
to the Pitthean deme,[3] if you know anyone from that deme called
Meletus, with long hair, not much of a beard, and a rather aquiline nose.

EUTHYPHRO: I don't know him, Socrates. What charge does he bring
against you?

---

1. We know nothing about Euthyphro except what we can gather from this
dialogue. He is obviously a professional priest who considers himself an expert
on ritual and on piety generally and, it seems, is generally so considered. One
Euthyphro is mentioned in Plato's *Cratylus* (396d) who is given to *enthousi-
asmos*, inspiration or possession, but we cannot be sure that it is the same person.

2. The Lyceum was an outdoor gymnasium, just outside the walls of Athens,
where teenage young men engaged in exercises and athletic competitions.
Socrates and other intellectuals carried on discussions with them there and
exhibited their skills. See the beginnings of Plato's *Euthydemus* and *Lysis*, and
the last paragraph of *Symposium*. The king-archon, one of the nine principal
magistrates of Athens, had the responsibility to oversee religious rituals and
purifications, and as such had oversight of legal cases involving alleged offenses
against the Olympian gods, whose worship was a civic function — it was regarded
as a serious offense to offend them.

3. A deme was, in effect, one of the constituent villages of Attica, the territory
whose center was the city of Athens (though Athens itself was divided into
demes, too). Athenian citizens had first of all to be enrolled and recognized
as citizens in their demes.

SOCRATES: What charge? A not ignoble one I think, for it is no small   c
thing for a young man to have knowledge of such an important subject.
He says he knows how our young men are corrupted and who corrupts
them. He is likely to be wise, and when he sees my ignorance corrupting
his contemporaries, he proceeds to accuse me to the city as to their
mother. I think he is the only one of our public men to start out the   d
right way, for it is right to care first that the young should be as good
as possible, just as a good farmer is likely to take care of the young
plants first, and of the others later. So, too, Meletus first gets rid of us
who corrupt the young shoots, as he says, and then afterwards he will   3
obviously take care of the older ones and become a source of great
blessings for the city, as seems likely to happen to one who started out
this way.

EUTHYPHRO: I could wish this were true, Socrates, but I fear the
opposite may happen. He seems to me to start out by harming the very
heart of the city by attempting to wrong you. Tell me, what does he
say you do to corrupt the young?

SOCRATES: Strange things, to hear him tell it, for he says that I am   b
a maker of gods, and on the ground that I create new gods while not
believing in the old gods, he has indicted me for their sake, as he puts it.

EUTHYPHRO: I understand, Socrates. This is because you say that the
divine sign keeps coming to you.[4] So he has written this indictment
against you as one who makes innovations in religious matters, and he
comes to court to slander you, knowing that such things are easily
misrepresented to the crowd. The same is true in my case. Whenever   c
I speak of divine matters in the assembly[5] and foretell the future, they
laugh me down as if I were crazy; and yet I have foretold nothing that
did not happen. Nevertheless, they envy all of us who do this. One
need not worry about them, but meet them head-on.

SOCRATES: My dear Euthyphro, to be laughed at does not matter
perhaps, for the Athenians do not mind anyone they think clever, as

---

4. In Plato, Socrates always speaks of his divine sign or voice as intervening to
prevent him from doing or saying something (e.g., *Apology* 31d), but never
positively. The popular view was that it enabled him to foretell the future, and
Euthyphro here represents that view. Note, however, that Socrates dissociates
himself from "you prophets" (3e).

5. The assembly was the final decision-making body of the Athenian democracy.
All adult males could attend and vote.

long as he does not teach his own wisdom, but if they think that he
d   makes others to be like himself they get angry, whether through envy,
as you say, or for some other reason.

EUTHYPHRO: I have certainly no desire to test their feelings towards
me in this matter.

SOCRATES: Perhaps you seem to make yourself but rarely available,
and not be willing to teach your own wisdom, but I'm afraid that my
liking for people makes them think that I pour out to anybody anything
I have to say, not only without charging a fee but even glad to reward
anyone who is willing to listen. If then they were intending to laugh
e   at me, as you say they laugh at you, there would be nothing unpleasant
in their spending their time in court laughing and jesting, but if they
are going to be serious, the outcome is not clear except to you prophets.

EUTHYPHRO: Perhaps it will come to nothing, Socrates, and you will
fight your case as you think best, as I think I will mine.

SOCRATES: What is your case, Euthyphro? Are you the defendant or
the prosecutor?

EUTHYPHRO: The prosecutor.

SOCRATES: Whom do you prosecute?

4   EUTHYPHRO: One whom I am thought crazy to prosecute.

SOCRATES: Are you pursuing someone who will easily escape you?

EUTHYPHRO: Far from it, for he is quite old.

SOCRATES: Who is it?

EUTHYPHRO: My father.

SOCRATES: My dear sir! Your own father?

EUTHYPHRO: Certainly.

SOCRATES: What is the charge? What is the case about?

EUTHYPHRO: Murder, Socrates.

SOCRATES: Good heavens! Certainly, Euthyphro, most men would
b   not know how they could do this and be right. It is not the part of
anyone to do this, but of one who is far advanced in wisdom.

EUTHYPHRO: Yes, by Zeus, Socrates, that is so.

SOCRATES: Is then the man your father killed one of your relatives?
Or is that obvious, for you would not prosecute your father for the
murder of a stranger.

EUTHYPHRO: It is ridiculous, Socrates, for you to think that it makes any difference whether the victim is a stranger or a relative. One should only watch whether the killer acted justly or not; if he acted justly, let him go, but if not, one should prosecute, if, that is to say, the killer c shares your hearth and table. The pollution is the same if you knowingly keep company with such a man and do not cleanse yourself and him by bringing him to justice. The victim was a dependent of mine, and when we were farming in Naxos he was a servant of ours.[6] He killed one of our household slaves in drunken anger, so my father bound him hand and foot and threw him in a ditch, then sent a man here to inquire from the priest what should be done. During that time he gave d no thought or care to the bound man, as being a killer, and it was no matter if he died, which he did. Hunger and cold and his bonds caused his death before the messenger came back from the seer. Both my father and my other relatives are angry that I am prosecuting my father for murder on behalf of a murderer when he hadn't even killed him, they say, and even if he had, the dead man does not deserve a thought, since he was a killer. For, they say, it is impious for a son to prosecute e his father for murder. But their ideas of the divine attitude to piety and impiety are wrong, Socrates.

SOCRATES: Whereas, by Zeus, Euthyphro, you think that your knowledge of the divine, and of piety and impiety, is so accurate that, when those things happened as you say, you have no fear of having acted impiously in bringing your father to trial?

EUTHYPHRO: I should be of no use, Socrates, and Euthyphro would not be superior to the majority of men, if I did not have accurate 5 knowledge of all such things.

SOCRATES: It is indeed most important, my admirable Euthyphro, that I should become your pupil, and as regards this indictment, challenge Meletus about these very things and say to him: that in the past too I considered knowledge about the divine to be most important, and that now that he says that I am guilty of improvising and innovating about the gods I have become your pupil. I would say to him: "If, Meletus, you agree that Euthyphro is wise in these matters, consider b me, too, to have the right beliefs and do not bring me to trial. If you

---

6. Naxos is a large island in the Aegean Sea southeast of Athens, where Athens had appropriated land and settled many of its citizens under its imperial rule in the mid–fifth century B.C.

do not think so, then prosecute that teacher of mine, not me, for corrupting the older men, me and his own father, by teaching me and by exhorting and punishing him." If he is not convinced, and does not discharge me or indict you instead of me, I shall repeat the same challenge in court.

EUTHYPHRO: Yes, by Zeus, Socrates, and, if he should try to indict
c me, I think I would find his weak spots and the talk in court would be about him rather than about me.

SOCRATES: It is because I realize this that I am eager to become your pupil, my dear friend. I know that other people as well as this Meletus do not even seem to notice you, whereas he sees me so sharply and clearly that he indicts me for ungodliness. So tell me now, by Zeus, what you just now maintained you clearly knew: what kind of thing do
d you say that godliness and ungodliness are, both as regards murder and other things; or is the pious not the same and alike in every action, and the impious the opposite of all that is pious and like itself, and everything that is to be impious presents us with one form[7] or appearance insofar as it is impious?

EUTHYPHRO: Most certainly, Socrates.

SOCRATES: Tell me then, what is the pious, and what the impious, do you say?

EUTHYPHRO: I say that the pious is to do what I am doing now, to prosecute the wrongdoer, be it about murder or temple robbery or
e anything else, whether the wrongdoer is your father or your mother or anyone else; not to prosecute is impious. And observe, Socrates, that I can cite powerful evidence that the law is so. I have already said to others that such actions are right, not to favor the ungodly, whoever they are. These people themselves believe that Zeus is the best and
6 most just of the gods, yet they agree that he bound his father because

---

7. This is the kind of passage that makes it easier for us to follow the transition from Socrates' universal definitions to the Platonic theory of separately existent eternal universal Forms. The words *eidos* and *idea*, the technical terms for the Platonic Forms, commonly mean physical stature or bodily appearance. As we apply a common epithet, in this case pious, to different actions or things, these must have a common characteristic, present a common appearance or form, to justify the use of the same term, but in the early dialogues, as here, it seems to be thought of as immanent in the particulars and without separate existence. The same is true of 6d where the word "form" is also used.

he unjustly swallowed his sons, and that he in turn castrated his father for similar reasons. But they are angry with me because I am prosecuting my father for his wrongdoing. They contradict themselves in what they say about the gods and about me.

SOCRATES: Indeed, Euthyphro, this is the reason why I am a defendant in the case, because I find it hard to accept things like that being said about the gods, and it is likely to be the reason why I shall be told I do wrong. Now, however, if you, who have full knowledge of such things, share their opinions, then we must agree with them, too, it would seem. For what are we to say, we who agree that we ourselves have no knowledge of them? Tell me, by the god of friendship, do you really believe these things are true?   b

EUTHYPHRO: Yes, Socrates, and so are even more surprising things, of which the majority has no knowledge.

SOCRATES: And do you believe that there really is war among the gods, and terrible enmities and battles, and other such things as are told by the poets, and other sacred stories such as are embroidered by good writers and by representations of which the robe of the goddess is adorned when it is carried up to the Acropolis?[8] Are we to say these things are true, Euthyphro?   c

EUTHYPHRO: Not only these, Socrates, but, as I was saying just now, I will, if you wish, relate many other things about the gods which I know will amaze you.

SOCRATES: I should not be surprised, but you will tell me these at leisure some other time. For now, try to tell me more clearly what I was asking just now, for, my friend, you did not teach me adequately when I asked you what the pious was, but you told me that what you are doing now, in prosecuting your father for murder, is pious.   d

EUTHYPHRO: And I told the truth, Socrates.

SOCRATES: Perhaps. You agree, however, that there are many other pious actions.

EUTHYPHRO: There are.

---

8. The Acropolis is the huge rocky outcropping in the center of Athens that served as the citadel for Attica, and also the center of its religious life. Major temples to the gods were there, including the Parthenon, the temple of Athena, the city's protectress. Every four years in an elaborate festival in her honor maidens brought up the ceremonial robe referred to here, in which to clothe her statue.

SOCRATES: Bear in mind then that I did not bid you tell me one or two of the many pious actions but that form itself that makes all pious actions pious, for you agreed that all impious actions are impious and

e   all pious actions pious through one form, or don't you remember?

EUTHYPHRO: I do.

SOCRATES: Tell me then what this form itself is, so that I may look upon it and, using it as a model, say that any action of yours or another's that is of that kind is pious, and if it is not that it is not.

EUTHYPHRO: If that is how you want it, Socrates, that is how I will tell you.

SOCRATES: That is what I want.

7   EUTHYPHRO: Well then, what is dear to the gods is pious, what is not is impious.

SOCRATES: Splendid, Euthyphro! You have now answered in the way I wanted. Whether your answer is true I do not know yet, but you will obviously show me that what you say is true.

EUTHYPHRO: Certainly.

SOCRATES: Come then, let us examine what we mean. An action or a man dear to the gods is pious, but an action or a man hated by the gods is impious. They are not the same, but quite opposite, the pious and the impious. Is that not so?

EUTHYPHRO: It is indeed.

SOCRATES: And that seems to be a good statement?

b   EUTHYPHRO: I think so, Socrates.

SOCRATES: We have also stated that the gods are in a state of discord, that they are at odds with each other, Euthyphro, and that they are at enmity with each other. Has that, too, been said?

EUTHYPHRO: It has.

SOCRATES: What are the subjects of difference that cause hatred and anger? Let us look at it this way. If you and I were to differ about numbers as to which is the greater, would this difference make us enemies and angry with each other, or would we proceed to count and

c   soon resolve our difference about this?

EUTHYPHRO: We would certainly do so.

SOCRATES: Again, if we differed about the larger and the smaller, we would turn to measurement and soon cease to differ.

EUTHYPHRO: That is so.

SOCRATES: And about the heavier and the lighter, we would resort to weighing and be reconciled.

EUTHYPHRO: Of course.

SOCRATES: What subject of difference would make us angry and hostile to each other if we were unable to come to a decision? Perhaps you do not have an answer ready, but examine as I tell you whether these subjects are the just and the unjust, the beautiful and the ugly, the good and the bad. Are these not the subjects of difference about which, when we are unable to come to a satisfactory decision, you and I and other men become hostile to each other whenever we do? d

EUTHYPHRO: That is the difference, Socrates, about those subjects.

SOCRATES: What about the gods, Euthyphro? If indeed they have differences, will it not be about these same subjects?

EUTHYPHRO: It certainly must be so.

SOCRATES: Then according to your argument, my good Euthyphro, different gods consider different things to be just, beautiful, ugly, good, and bad, for they would not be at odds with one another unless they differed about these subjects, would they? e

EUTHYPHRO: You are right.

SOCRATES: And they like what each of them considers beautiful, good, and just, and hate the opposites of these?

EUTHYPHRO: Certainly.

SOCRATES: But you say that the same things are considered just by some gods and unjust by others, and as they dispute about these things they are at odds and at war with each other. Is that not so? 8

EUTHYPHRO: It is.

SOCRATES: The same things then are loved by the gods and hated by the gods, and would be both god-loved and god-hated.

EUTHYPHRO: It seems likely.

SOCRATES: And the same things would be both pious and impious, according to this argument?

EUTHYPHRO: I'm afraid so.

SOCRATES: So you did not answer my question, you surprising man. I did not ask you what same thing is both pious and impious, and it appears that what is loved by the gods is also hated by them. So it is in no way surprising if your present action, namely punishing your b father, may be pleasing to Zeus but displeasing to Cronus and Uranus,[9] pleasing to Hephaestus but displeasing to Hera, and so with any other gods who differ from each other on this subject.

EUTHYPHRO: I think, Socrates, that on this subject no gods would differ from one another, that whoever has killed anyone unjustly should pay the penalty.

c   SOCRATES: Well now, Euthyphro, have you ever heard any man maintaining that one who has killed or done anything else unjustly should not pay the penalty?

EUTHYPHRO: They never cease to dispute on this subject, both elsewhere and in the courts, for when they have committed many wrongs they do and say anything to avoid the penalty.

SOCRATES: Do they agree they have done wrong, Euthyphro, and in spite of so agreeing do they nevertheless say they should not be punished?

EUTHYPHRO: No, they do not agree on that point.

SOCRATES: So they do not say or do just anything. For they do not venture to say this, or dispute that they must not pay the penalty if they d   have done wrong, but I think they deny doing wrong. Is that not so?

EUTHYPHRO: That is true.

SOCRATES: Then they do not dispute that the wrongdoer must be punished, but they may disagree as to who the wrongdoer is, what he did, and when.

EUTHYPHRO: You are right.

SOCRATES: Do not the gods have the same experience, if indeed they are at odds with each other about the just and the unjust, as your argument maintains? Some assert that they wrong one another, while e   others deny it, but no one among gods or men ventures to say that the wrongdoer must not be punished.

EUTHYPHRO: Yes, that is true, Socrates, as to the main point.

SOCRATES: And those who disagree, whether men or gods, dispute about each action, if indeed the gods disagree. Some say it is done justly, others unjustly. Is that not so?

---

9. Zeus' father, whom he fought and defeated (see 6a), was Cronus; Cronus, in turn, had castrated his own father Uranus. The story of Hephaestus and his mother Hera, mentioned next, similarly involves a son punishing his parent.

EUTHYPHRO: Yes, indeed.

SOCRATES: Come now, my dear Euthyphro, tell me, too, that I may   9
become wiser, what proof you have that all the gods consider that man
to have been killed unjustly who became a murderer while in your
service, was bound by the master of his victim, and died in his bonds
before the one who bound him found out from the seers what was to
be done with him, and that it is right for a son to denounce and to
prosecute his father on behalf of such a man. Come, try to show me
a clear sign that all the gods definitely believe this action to be right.   b
If you can give me adequate proof of this, I shall never cease to extol
your wisdom.

EUTHYPHRO: This is perhaps no light task, Socrates, though I could
show you very clearly.

SOCRATES: I understand that you think me more dull-witted than
the jury, as you will obviously show them that these actions were unjust
and that all the gods hate such actions.

EUTHYPHRO: I will show it to them clearly, Socrates, if only they will
listen to me.

SOCRATES: They will listen if they think you show them well. But   c
this thought came to me as you were speaking, and I am examining
it, saying to myself: "If Euthyphro shows me conclusively that all the
gods consider such a death unjust, to what greater extent have I learned
from him the nature of piety and impiety? This action would then, it
seems, be hated by the gods, but the pious and the impious were not
thereby now defined, for what is hated by the gods has also been shown
to be loved by them." So I will not insist on this point; let us assume,
if you wish, that all the gods consider this unjust and that they all hate   d
it. However, is this the correction we are making in our discussion,
that what all the gods hate is impious, and what they all love is pious,
and that what some gods love and others hate is neither or both? Is
that how you now wish us to define piety and impiety?

EUTHYPHRO: What prevents us from doing so, Socrates?

SOCRATES: For my part nothing, Euthyphro, but you look whether
on your part this proposal will enable you to teach me most easily what
you promised.

EUTHYPHRO: I would certainly say that the pious is what all the gods   e
love, and the opposite, what all the gods hate, is the impious.

SOCRATES: Then let us again examine whether that is a sound statement, or do we let it pass, and if one of us, or someone else, merely

says that something is so, do we accept that it is so? Or should we examine what the speaker means?

EUTHYPHRO: We must examine it, but I certainly think that this is now a fine statement.

10   SOCRATES: We shall soon know better whether it is. Consider this: Is the pious being loved by the gods because it is pious, or is it pious because it is being loved by the gods?

EUTHYPHRO: I don't know what you mean, Socrates.

SOCRATES: I shall try to explain more clearly: we speak of something carried and something carrying, of something led and something leading, of something seen and something seeing, and you understand that these things are all different from one another and how they differ?

EUTHYPHRO: I think I do.

SOCRATES: So there is also something loved and—a different thing—something loving.

EUTHYPHRO: Of course.

b   SOCRATES: Tell me then whether the thing carried is a carried thing because it is being carried, or for some other reason?

EUTHYPHRO: No, that is the reason.

SOCRATES: And the thing led is so because it is being led, and the thing seen because it is being seen?

EUTHYPHRO: Certainly.

SOCRATES: It is not being seen because it is a thing seen but on the contrary it is a thing seen because it is being seen; nor is it because it is something led that it is being led but because it is being led that it is something led; nor is something being carried because it is something carried, but it is something carried because it is being carried. Is what

c   I want to say clear, Euthyphro? I want to say this, namely, that if anything is being changed or is being affected in any way, it is not being changed because it is something changed, but rather it is something changed because it is being changed; nor is it being affected because it is something affected, but it is something affected because it is being affected.[10] Or do you not agree?

_____

10. Here Socrates gives the general principle under which, he says, the specific cases already examined—those of leading, carrying, and seeing—all fall. It is by being changed by something that changes *it* (e.g., by carrying it somewhere) that anything is a changed thing—not vice versa: it is not by something's being a changed thing that something *else* then changes it so that it comes to be

EUTHYPHRO: I do.

SOCRATES: Is something loved either something changed or something affected by something?

EUTHYPHRO: Certainly.

SOCRATES: So it is in the same case as the things just mentioned; it is not being loved by those who love it because it is something loved, but it is something loved because it is being loved by them?

EUTHYPHRO: Necessarily.

SOCRATES: What then do we say about the pious, Euthyphro? Surely that it is being loved by all the gods, according to what you say?

EUTHYPHRO: Yes.

SOCRATES: Is it being loved because it is pious, or for some other reason?

EUTHYPHRO: For no other reason.

SOCRATES: It is being loved then because it is pious, but it is not pious because it is being loved?

EUTHYPHRO: Apparently.

SOCRATES: And yet it is something loved and god-loved because it is being loved by the gods?

EUTHYPHRO: Of course.

SOCRATES: Then the god-loved is not the same as the pious, Euthyphro, nor the pious the same as the god-loved, as you say it is, but one differs from the other.

EUTHYPHRO: How so, Socrates?

SOCRATES: Because we agree that the pious is being loved for this reason, that it is pious, but it is not pious because it is being loved. Is that not so?

EUTHYPHRO: Yes.

SOCRATES: And that the god-loved, on the other hand, is so because it is being loved by the gods, by the very fact of being loved, but it is not being loved because it is god-loved.

EUTHYPHRO: True.

---

being changed (e.g., by carrying it somewhere). Likewise for "affections" such as being seen by someone: it is by being "affected" by something that "affects" it that anything is an "affected" thing, not vice versa. It is not by being an "affected" thing (e.g., a thing seen) that something else then "affects" it.

SOCRATES: But if the god-loved and the pious were the same, my dear Euthyphro, then if the pious was being loved because it was pious, the god-loved would also be being loved because it was god-loved; and if the god-loved was god-loved because it was being loved by the gods, then the pious would also be pious because it was being loved by the gods. But now you see that they are in opposite cases as being altogether different from each other: the one is such as to be loved because it is being loved, the other is being loved because it is such as to be loved. I'm afraid, Euthyphro, that when you were asked what piety is, you did not wish to make its nature clear to me, but you told me an affect or a quality of it, that the pious has the quality of being loved by all the gods, but you have not yet told me what the pious is. Now, if you will, do not hide things from me but tell me again from the beginning what piety is, whether being loved by the gods or having some other quality— we shall not quarrel about that—but be keen to tell me what the pious and the impious are.

EUTHYPHRO: But Socrates, I have no way of telling you what I have in mind, for whatever proposition we put forward goes around and refuses to stay put where we establish it.

SOCRATES: Your statements, Euthyphro, seem to belong to my ancestor, Daedalus.[11] If I were stating them and putting them forward, you would perhaps be making fun of me and say that because of my kinship with him my conclusions in discussion run away and will not stay where one puts them. As these propositions are yours, however, we need some other jest, for they will not stay put for you, as you say yourself.

EUTHYPHRO: I think the same jest will do for our discussion, Socrates, for I am not the one who makes them go around and not remain in the same place; it is you who are the Daedalus; for as far as I am concerned they would remain as they were.

SOCRATES: It looks as if I was cleverer than Daedalus in using my skill, my friend, insofar as he could only cause to move the things he made himself, but I can make other people's things move as well as my own. And the smartest part of my skill is that I am clever without wanting to be, for I would rather have your statements to me remain unmoved than possess the wealth of Tantalus as well as the cleverness of Daedalus. But enough of this. Since I think you are making unnecessary

---

11. Socrates may have been a stonemason, as his father was. In Greek mythology Daedalus' statues (made of wood) could move themselves.

difficulties, I am as eager as you are to find a way to teach me about piety, and do not give up before you do. See whether you think all that is pious is of necessity just.

EUTHYPHRO: I think so.

SOCRATES: And is then all that is just pious? Or is all that is pious just, but not all that is just pious, but some of it is and some is not?   12

EUTHYPHRO: I do not follow what you are saying, Socrates.

SOCRATES: Yet you are younger than I by as much as you are wiser. As I say, you are making difficulties because of your wealth of wisdom. Pull yourself together, my dear sir, what I am saying is not difficult to grasp. I am saying the opposite of what the poet said who wrote:

> You do not wish to name Zeus, who had done it, and who made all
> things grow, for where there is fear there is also shame.[12]   b

I disagree with the poet. Shall I tell you why?

EUTHYPHRO: Please do.

SOCRATES: I do not think that "where there is fear there is also shame," for I think that many people who fear disease and poverty and many other such things feel fear, but are not ashamed of the things they fear. Do you not think so?

EUTHYPHRO: I do indeed.

SOCRATES: But where there is shame there is also fear. For is there anyone who, in feeling shame and embarrassment at anything, does   c
not also at the same time fear and dread a reputation for wickedness?

EUTHYPHRO: He is certainly afraid.

SOCRATES: It is then not right to say "where there is fear there is also shame," but that where there is shame there is also fear, for fear covers a larger area than shame. Shame is a part of fear just as odd is a part of number, with the result that it is not true that where there is number there is also oddness, but that where there is oddness there is also number. Do you follow me now?

EUTHYPHRO: Surely.

SOCRATES: This is the kind of thing I was asking before, whether where there is piety there is also justice, but where there is justice there   d
is not always piety, for the pious is a part of justice. Shall we say that, or do you think otherwise?

---

12. Author unknown.

EUTHYPHRO: No, but like that, for what you say appears to be right.

SOCRATES: See what comes next: if the pious is a part of the just, we must, it seems, find out what part of the just it is. Now if you asked me something of what we mentioned just now, such as what part of number is the even, and what number that is, I would say it is the number that is divisible into two equal, not unequal, parts. Or do you not think so?

EUTHYPHRO: I do.

e   SOCRATES: Try in this way to tell me what part of the just the pious is, in order to tell Meletus not to wrong us any more and not to indict me for ungodliness, since I have learned from you sufficiently what is godly and pious and what is not.

EUTHYPHRO: I think, Socrates, that the godly and pious is the part of the just that is concerned with the care of the gods, while that concerned with the care of men is the remaining part of justice.

13   SOCRATES: You seem to me to put that very well, but I still need a bit of information. I do not know yet what you mean by care, for you do not mean the care of the gods in the same sense as the care of other things, as, for example, we say, don't we, that not everyone knows how to care for horses, but the horse breeder does.

EUTHYPHRO: Yes, I do mean it that way.

SOCRATES: So horse breeding is the care of horses.

EUTHYPHRO: Yes.

SOCRATES: Nor does everyone know how to care for dogs, but the hunter does.

EUTHYPHRO: That is so.

SOCRATES: So hunting is the care of dogs.

b   EUTHYPHRO: Yes.

SOCRATES: And cattle raising is the care of cattle.

EUTHYPHRO: Quite so.

SOCRATES: While piety and godliness is the care of the gods, Euthyphro. Is that what you mean?

EUTHYPHRO: It is.

SOCRATES: Now care in each case has the same effect; it aims at the good and the benefit of the object cared for, as you can see that horses cared for by horse breeders are benefited and become better. Or do you not think so?

EUTHYPHRO: I do.

SOCRATES: So dogs are benefited by dog breeding, cattle by cattle raising, and so with all the others. Or do you think that care aims to harm the object of its care?   c

EUTHYPHRO: By Zeus, no.

SOCRATES: It aims to benefit the object of its care?

EUTHYPHRO: Of course.

SOCRATES: Is piety then, which is the care of the gods, also to benefit the gods and make them better? Would you agree that when you do something pious you make some one of the gods better?

EUTHYPHRO: By Zeus, no.

SOCRATES: Nor do I think that this is what you mean — far from it — but that is why I asked you what you meant by the care of gods, because I did not believe you meant this kind of care.   d

EUTHYPHRO: Quite right, Socrates, that is not the kind of care I mean.

SOCRATES: Very well, but what kind of care of the gods would piety be?

EUTHYPHRO: The kind of care, Socrates, that slaves take of their masters.

SOCRATES: I understand. It is likely to be a kind of service of the gods.

EUTHYPHRO: Quite so.

SOCRATES: Could you tell me to the achievement of what goal service to doctors tends? Is it not, do you think, to achieving health?

EUTHYPHRO: I think so.

SOCRATES: What about service to shipbuilders? To what achievement   e
is it directed?

EUTHYPHRO: Clearly, Socrates, to the building of a ship.

SOCRATES: And service to housebuilders to the building of a house?

EUTHYPHRO: Yes.

SOCRATES: Tell me then, my good sir, to the achievement of what aim does service to the gods tend? You obviously know since you say that you, of all men, have the best knowledge of the divine.

EUTHYPHRO: And I am telling the truth, Socrates.

SOCRATES: Tell me then, by Zeus, what is that excellent aim that the gods achieve, using us as their servants?

EUTHYPHRO: Many fine things, Socrates.

14   SOCRATES: So do generals, my friend. Nevertheless you could easily
tell me their main concern, which is to achieve victory in war, is it not?

EUTHYPHRO: Of course.

SOCRATES: The farmers, too, I think, achieve many fine things, but
the main point of their efforts is to produce food from the earth.

EUTHYPHRO: Quite so.

SOCRATES: Well then, how would you sum up the many fine things
that the gods achieve?

EUTHYPHRO: I told you a short while ago, Socrates, that it is a
b   considerable task to acquire any precise knowledge of these things, but,
to put it simply, I say that if a man knows how to say and do what is
pleasing to the gods at prayer and sacrifice, those are pious actions such
as preserve both private houses and public affairs of state. The opposite of
these pleasing actions are impious and overturn and destroy everything.

SOCRATES: You could tell me in far fewer words, if you were willing,
c   the sum of what I asked, Euthyphro, but you are not keen to teach me,
that is clear. You were on the point of doing so, but you turned away.
If you had given that answer, I should now have acquired from you
sufficient knowledge of the nature of piety. As it is, the lover of inquiry
must follow his beloved wherever it may lead him. Once more then,
what do you say that piety and the pious are? Are they a knowledge of
how to sacrifice and pray?

EUTHYPHRO: They are.

SOCRATES: To sacrifice is to make a gift to the gods, whereas to pray
is to beg from the gods?

EUTHYPHRO: Definitely, Socrates.

d   SOCRATES: It would follow from this statement that piety would be
a knowledge of how to give to, and beg from, the gods.

EUTHYPHRO: You understood what I said very well, Socrates.

SOCRATES: That is because I am so desirous of your wisdom, and I
concentrate my mind on it, so that no word of yours may fall to the
ground. But tell me, what is this service to the gods? You say it is to
beg from them and to give to them?

EUTHYPHRO: I do.

SOCRATES: And to beg correctly would be to ask from them things
that we need?

EUTHYPHRO: What else?

SOCRATES: And to give correctly is to give them what they need from us, for it would not be skillful to bring gifts to anyone that are in no way needed.

EUTHYPHRO: True, Socrates.

SOCRATES: Piety would then be a sort of trading skill between gods and men?

EUTHYPHRO: Trading yes, if you prefer to call it that.

SOCRATES: I prefer nothing, unless it is true. But tell me, what benefit do the gods derive from the gifts they receive from us? What they give us is obvious to all. There is for us no good that we do not receive from them, but how are they benefited by what they receive from us? Or do we have such an advantage over them in the trade that we receive all our blessings from them and they receive nothing from us?

EUTHYPHRO: Do you suppose, Socrates, that the gods are benefited by what they receive from us?

SOCRATES: What could those gifts from us to the gods be, Euthyphro?

EUTHYPHRO: What else, do you think, than honor, reverence, and what I mentioned just now, to please them?

SOCRATES: The pious is then, Euthyphro, pleasing to the gods, but not beneficial or dear to them?

EUTHYPHRO: I think it is of all things most dear to them.

SOCRATES: So the pious is once again what is dear to the gods.

EUTHYPHRO: Most certainly.

SOCRATES: When you say this, will you be surprised if your arguments seem to move about instead of staying put? And will you accuse me of being Daedalus who makes them move, though you are yourself much more skillful than Daedalus and make them go around in a circle? Or do you not realize that our argument has moved around and come again to the same place? You surely remember that earlier the pious and the god-loved were shown not to be the same but different from each other. Or do you not remember?

EUTHYPHRO: I do.

SOCRATES: Do you then not realize now that you are saying that what is dear to the gods is the pious? Is this not the same as the god-loved? Or is it not?

EUTHYPHRO: It certainly is.

SOCRATES: Either we were wrong when we agreed before, or, if we were right then, we are wrong now.

EUTHYPHRO: That seems to be so.

SOCRATES: So we must investigate again from the beginning what piety is, as I shall not willingly give up before I learn this. Do not think me unworthy, but concentrate your attention and tell the truth. For you know it, if any man does, and I must not let you go, like Proteus,[13] before you tell me. If you had no clear knowledge of piety and impiety you would never have ventured to prosecute your old father for murder on behalf of a servant. For fear of the gods you would have been afraid to take the risk lest you should not be acting rightly, and would have been ashamed before men, but now I know well that you believe you have clear knowledge of piety and impiety. So tell me, my good Euthyphro, and do not hide what you think it is.

EUTHYPHRO: Some other time, Socrates, for I am in a hurry now, and it is time for me to go.

SOCRATES: What a thing to do, my friend! By going you have cast me down from a great hope I had, that I would learn from you the nature of the pious and the impious and so escape Meletus' indictment by showing him that I had acquired wisdom in divine matters from Euthyphro, and my ignorance would no longer cause me to be careless and inventive about such things, and that I would be better for the rest of my life.

---

13. In Greek mythology Proteus was a sort of old man of the sea, who could keep on changing his form and so escape being questioned. See Homer, *Odyssey* iv.382 ff.

APOLOGY

The Apology[1] *professes to be a record of the actual speech that*
Socrates delivered in his own defense at the trial. This claim makes the
question of its historicity more acute than in the dialogues in which
the conversations themselves are mostly fictional and the question of
historicity is concerned only with how far the theories that Socrates is
represented as expressing were those of the historical Socrates. Here,
however, we are dealing with a speech that Socrates made as a matter
of history. How far is Plato's account accurate? We should always
remember that the ancients did not expect historical accuracy in the
way we do. On the other hand, Plato makes it clear that he was
present at the trial (34a, 38b). Moreover, if, as is generally believed,
the Apology *was written not long after the event, many Athenians*
would remember the actual speech, and it would be a poor way to
vindicate the Master, which is the obvious intent, to put a completely
different speech into his mouth. Some liberties could no doubt be
allowed, but the main arguments and the general tone of the defense
must surely be faithful to the original. The beauty of language and
style is certainly Plato's, but the serene spiritual and moral beauty of
character belongs to Socrates. It is a powerful combination.

Athenian juries were very large, in this case 501, and they
combined the duties of jury and judge as we know them by both
convicting and sentencing. Obviously, it would have been virtually
impossible for so large a body to discuss various penalties and decide
on one. The problem was resolved rather neatly, however, by having
the prosecutor, after conviction, assess the penalty he thought
appropriate, followed by a counter-assessment by the defendant. The
jury would then decide between the two. This procedure generally
made for moderation on both sides.

Thus the Apology *is in three parts. The first and major part is the*
main speech (17a–35d), followed by the counter-assessment (35e–38b),

---

1. The word *apology* is a transliteration, not a translation, of the Greek *apologia*,
which means defense. There is certainly nothing apologetic about the speech.

and finally, last words to the jury (38c–42a), both to those who voted for the death sentence and those who voted for acquittal.

G.M.A.G.

17 I do not know, men of Athens,[2] how my accusers affected you; as for me, I was almost carried away in spite of myself, so persuasively did they speak. And yet, hardly anything of what they said is true. Of the many lies they told, one in particular surprised me, namely that you should be careful not to be deceived by an accomplished speaker like
b me. That they were not ashamed to be immediately proved wrong by the facts, when I show myself not to be an accomplished speaker at all, that I thought was most shameless on their part—unless indeed they call an accomplished speaker the man who speaks the truth. If they mean that, I would agree that I am an orator, but not after their manner, for indeed, as I say, practically nothing they said was true. From me you will hear the whole truth, though not, by Zeus, gentlemen,
c expressed in embroidered and stylized phrases like theirs, but things spoken at random and expressed in the first words that come to mind, for I put my trust in the justice of what I say, and let none of you expect anything else. It would not be fitting at my age, as it might be for a young man, to toy with words when I appear before you.

One thing I do ask and beg of you, gentlemen: if you hear me making my defense in the same kind of language as I am accustomed to use in the marketplace by the bankers' tables,[3] where many of you
d have heard me, and elsewhere, do not be surprised or create a distur-

---

2. Jurors were selected by lot from all the male citizens thirty years of age or older who offered themselves on the given day for service. They thus functioned as representatives of the Athenian people and the Athenian democracy. In cases like Socrates', they judged on behalf of the whole citizen body whether or not their interests had been undermined by the accused's behavior. Hence Socrates can address them as if he were addressing the people of Athens at large, and in particular the partisans of the democracy against its oligarchic opponents (see, for example, 21a, 32d). Socrates addresses the jury as "men of Athens" rather than employing the usual mode of address, "gentlemen of the jury" (as Meletus does at 26d). At 40a he explains that only those who voted to acquit him deserved that honor.

3. The bankers or money-changers had their counters in the marketplace. It seems that this was a favorite place for gossip.

bance on that account. The position is this: This is my first appearance
in a lawcourt, at the age of seventy; I am therefore simply a stranger
to the manner of speaking here. Just as if I were really a stranger, you
would certainly excuse me if I spoke in that dialect and manner in
which I had been brought up, so too my present request seems a just   18
one, for you to pay no attention to my manner of speech—be it better
or worse—but to concentrate your attention on whether what I say is
just or not, for the excellence of a judge lies in this, as that of a speaker
lies in telling the truth.

It is right for me, gentlemen, to defend myself first against the first
lying accusations made against me and my first accusers, and then
against the later accusations and the later accusers. There have been
many who have accused me to you for many years now, and none of   b
their accusations are true. These I fear much more than I fear Anytus
and his friends, though they too are formidable. These earlier ones,
however, are more so, gentlemen; they got hold of most of you from
childhood, persuaded you and accused me quite falsely, saying that
there is a man called Socrates, a wise man, a student of all things in
the sky and below the earth, who makes the worse argument the
stronger. Those who spread that rumor, gentlemen, are my dangerous   c
accusers, for their hearers believe that those who study these things do
not even believe in the gods. Moreover, these accusers are numerous,
and have been at it a long time; also, they spoke to you at an age
when you would most readily believe them, some of you being children
and adolescents, and they won their case by default, as there was
no defense.

What is most absurd in all this is that one cannot even know or
mention their names unless one of them is a writer of comedies.[4] Those   d
who maliciously and slanderously persuaded you—who also, when
persuaded themselves then persuaded others—all those are most difficult to deal with: one cannot bring one of them into court or refute
him; one must simply fight with shadows, as it were, in making one's
defense, and cross-examine when no one answers. I want you to realize
too that my accusers are of two kinds: those who have accused me
recently, and the old ones I mention; and to think that I must first
defend myself against the latter, for you have also heard their accusations   e
first, and to a much greater extent than the more recent.

---

4. This is Aristophanes. Socrates refers below (19c) to the character Socrates
in his *Clouds* (225 ff.), first produced in 423 B.C.

Very well then, men of Athens. I must surely defend myself and
19 attempt to uproot from your minds in so short a time the slander that
has resided there so long. I wish this may happen, if it is in any way
better for you and me, and that my defense may be successful, but I
think this is very difficult and I am fully aware of how difficult it is.
Even so, let the matter proceed as the god may wish, but I must obey
the law and make my defense.

Let us then take up the case from its beginning. What is the accusa-
b tion from which arose the slander in which Meletus trusted when he
wrote out the charge against me? What did they say when they slandered
me? I must, as if they were my actual prosecutors, read the affidavit
they would have sworn. It goes something like this: Socrates is guilty
of wrongdoing in that he busies himself studying things in the sky and
below the earth; he makes the worse into the stronger argument, and
c he teaches these same things to others. You have seen this yourself in
the comedy of Aristophanes, a Socrates swinging about there, saying
he was walking on air and talking a lot of other nonsense about things
of which I know nothing at all. I do not speak in contempt of such
knowledge, if someone is wise in these things—lest Meletus bring more
cases against me—but, gentlemen, I have no part in it, and on this
point I call upon the majority of you as witnesses. I think it right that
d all those of you who have heard me conversing, and many of you have,
should tell each other if any one of you has ever heard me discussing
such subjects to any extent at all. From this you will learn that the
other things said about me by the majority are of the same kind.

Not one of them is true. And if you have heard from anyone that I
undertake to teach people and charge a fee for it, that is not true either.
e Yet I think it a fine thing to be able to teach people as Gorgias of
Leontini does, and Prodicus of Ceos, and Hippias of Elis.[5] Each of
these men can go to any city and persuade the young, who can keep
company with any one of their own fellow citizens they want without
20 paying, to leave the company of these, to join with themselves, pay

---

5. These were all well-known Sophists. Gorgias, after whom Plato named one
of his dialogues, was a celebrated rhetorician and teacher of rhetoric. He came
to Athens in 427 B.C., and his rhetorical tricks took the city by storm. Two
dialogues, the authenticity of which has been doubted, are named after Hippias,
whose knowledge was encyclopedic. Prodicus was known for his insistence on
the precise meaning of words. Both he and Hippias are characters in *Protagoras*
(named after another famous Sophist).

them a fee, and be grateful to them besides. Indeed, I learned that there is another wise man from Paros who is visiting us, for I met a man who has spent more money on sophists than everybody else put together, Callias, the son of Hipponicus. So I asked him—he has two sons—"Callias," I said, "if your sons were colts or calves, we could find and engage a supervisor for them who would make them excel in their proper qualities, some horse breeder or farmer. Now since they are   b
men, whom do you have in mind to supervise them? Who is an expert in this kind of excellence, the human and social kind? I think you must have given thought to this since you have sons. Is there such a person," I asked, "or is there not?" "Certainly there is," he said. "Who is he?" I asked. "What is his name, where is he from? And what is his fee?" "His name, Socrates, is Evenus, he comes from Paros, and his fee is five minas."[6] I thought Evenus a happy man, if he really possesses this art, and teaches for so moderate a fee. Certainly I would pride and preen   c
myself if I had this knowledge, but I do not have it, gentlemen.

One of you might perhaps interrupt me and say: "But Socrates, what is your occupation? From where have these slanders come? For surely if you did not busy yourself with something out of the common, all these rumors and talk would not have arisen unless you did something other than most people. Tell us what it is, that we may not speak inadvisedly about you." Anyone who says that seems to be right, and I   d
will try to show you what has caused this reputation and slander. Listen then. Perhaps some of you will think I am jesting, but be sure that all that I shall say is true. What has caused my reputation is none other than a certain kind of wisdom. What kind of wisdom? Human wisdom, perhaps. It may be that I really possess this, while those whom I mentioned just now are wise with a wisdom more than human; else I cannot   e
explain it, for I certainly do not possess it, and whoever says I do is lying and speaks to slander me. Do not create a disturbance, gentlemen, even if you think I am boasting, for the story I shall tell does not originate with me, but I will refer you to a trustworthy source. I shall call upon the god at Delphi as witness to the existence and nature of   21
my wisdom, if it be such.[7] You know Chaerephon. He was my friend from youth, and the friend of most of you, as he shared your exile and

---

6. A mina equaled 100 drachmas. In Socrates' time one drachma was the daily wage of a day-laborer. So Evenus' fee was a considerable sum.

7. The god Apollo had a very famous shrine at Delphi, where his oracles were delivered through the mouth of a priestess, the "Pythian."

your return. You surely know the kind of man he was, how impulsive in any course of action. He went to Delphi at one time and ventured to ask the oracle—as I say, gentlemen, do not create a disturbance—he asked if any man was wiser than I, and the Pythian replied that no one was wiser. Chaerephon is dead, but his brother will testify to you about this.

b   Consider that I tell you this because I would inform you about the origin of the slander. When I heard of this reply I asked myself: "Whatever does the god mean? What is his riddle? I am very conscious that I am not wise at all; what then does he mean by saying that I am the wisest? For surely he does not lie; it is not legitimate for him to do so." For a long time I was at a loss as to his meaning; then I very reluctantly turned to some such investigation as this; I went to one of those reputed

c   wise, thinking that there, if anywhere, I could refute the oracle and say to it: "This man is wiser than I, but you said I was." Then, when I examined this man—there is no need for me to tell you his name, he was one of our public men—my experience was something like this: I thought that he appeared wise to many people and especially to himself,

d   but he was not. I then tried to show him that he thought himself wise, but that he was not. As a result he came to dislike me, and so did many of the bystanders. So I withdrew and thought to myself: "I am wiser than this man; it is likely that neither of us knows anything worthwhile, but he thinks he knows something when he does not, whereas when I do not know, neither do I think I know; so I am likely to be wiser than he to this small extent, that I do not think I know what I do not know."

e   After this I approached another man, one of those thought to be wiser than he, and I thought the same thing, and so I came to be disliked both by him and by many others.

       After that I proceeded systematically. I realized, to my sorrow and alarm, that I was getting unpopular, but I thought that I must attach the greatest importance to the god's oracle, so I must go to all those who had any reputation for knowledge to examine its meaning. And

22   by the dog,[8] men of Athens—for I must tell you the truth—I experienced something like this: In my investigation in the service of the god I found that those who had the highest reputation were nearly the most deficient, while those who were thought to be inferior were more knowledgeable. I must give you an account of my journeyings as if they

---

8. A curious oath, occasionally used by Socrates, it appears in a longer form in *Gorgias* (482b) as "by the dog, the god of the Egyptians."

were labors I had undertaken to prove the oracle irrefutable. After the politicians, I went to the poets, the writers of tragedies and dithyrambs and the others, intending in their case to catch myself being more ignorant than they. So I took up those poems with which they seemed to have taken most trouble and asked them what they meant, in order that I might at the same time learn something from them. I am ashamed to tell you the truth, gentlemen, but I must. Almost all the bystanders might have explained the poems better than their authors could. I soon realized that poets do not compose their poems with knowledge, but by some inborn talent and by inspiration, like seers and prophets who also say many fine things without any understanding of what they say. The poets seemed to me to have had a similar experience. At the same time I saw that, because of their poetry, they thought themselves very wise men in other respects, which they were not. So there again I withdrew, thinking that I had the same advantage over them as I had over the politicians.

Finally I went to the craftsmen, for I was conscious of knowing practically nothing, and I knew that I would find that they had knowledge of many fine things. In this I was not mistaken; they knew things I did not know, and to that extent they were wiser than I. But, men of Athens, the good craftsmen seemed to me to have the same fault as the poets: each of them, because of his success at his craft, thought himself very wise in other most important pursuits, and this error of theirs overshadowed the wisdom they had, so that I asked myself, on behalf of the oracle, whether I should prefer to be as I am, with neither their wisdom nor their ignorance, or to have both. The answer I gave myself and the oracle was that it was to my advantage to be as I am.

As a result of this investigation, men of Athens, I acquired much unpopularity, of a kind that is hard to deal with and is a heavy burden; many slanders came from these people and a reputation for wisdom, for in each case the bystanders thought that I myself possessed the wisdom that I proved that my interlocutor did not have. What is probable, gentlemen, is that in fact the god is wise and that his oracular response meant that human wisdom is worth little or nothing, and that when he says this man, Socrates, he is using my name as an example, as if he said: "This man among you, mortals, is wisest who, like Socrates, understands that his wisdom is worthless." So even now I continue this investigation as the god bade me—and I go around seeking out anyone, citizen or stranger, whom I think wise. Then if I do not think he is, I come to the assistance of the god and show him that he is not wise.

Because of this occupation, I do not have the leisure to engage in public affairs to any extent, nor indeed to look after my own, but I live in great poverty because of my service to the god.

c   Furthermore, the young men who follow me around of their own free will, those who have most leisure, the sons of the very rich, take pleasure in hearing people questioned; they themselves often imitate me and try to question others. I think they find an abundance of men who believe they have some knowledge but know little or nothing. The result is that those whom they question are angry, not with themselves

d   but with me. They say: "That man Socrates is a pestilential fellow who corrupts the young." If one asks them what he does and what he teaches to corrupt them, they are silent, as they do not know, but, so as not to appear at a loss, they mention those accusations that are available against all philosophers, about "things in the sky and things below the earth," about "not believing in the gods" and "making the worse the stronger argument"; they would not want to tell the truth, I'm sure, that they have been proved to lay claim to knowledge when they know nothing.

e   These people are ambitious, violent, and numerous; they are continually and convincingly talking about me; they have been filling your ears for a long time with vehement slanders against me. From them Meletus attacked me, and Anytus and Lycon, Meletus being vexed on behalf of the poets, Anytus on behalf of the craftsmen and the politicians,

24   Lycon on behalf of the orators, so that, as I started out by saying, I should be surprised if I could rid you of so much slander in so short a time. That, men of Athens, is the truth for you. I have hidden or disguised nothing. I know well enough that this very conduct makes

b   me unpopular, and this is proof that what I say is true, that such is the slander against me, and that such are its causes. If you look into this either now or later, this is what you will find.

Let this suffice as a defense against the charges of my earlier accusers. After this I shall try to defend myself against Meletus, that good and patriotic man, as he says he is, and my later accusers. As these are a different lot of accusers, let us again take up their sworn deposition. It goes something like this: Socrates is guilty of corrupting the young and of not believing in the gods in whom the city believes, but in other

c   new spiritual things. Such is their charge. Let us examine it point by point.

He says that I am guilty of corrupting the young, but I say that Meletus is guilty of dealing frivolously with serious matters, of irresponsibly bringing people into court, and of professing to be seriously concerned with things about none of which he has ever cared, and I shall try to prove that this is so. Come here and tell me, Meletus. Surely you consider it of the greatest importance that our young men be as good as possible?[9] — Indeed I do.   d

Come then, tell these men who improves them. You obviously know, in view of your concern. You say you have discovered the one who corrupts them, namely me, and you bring me here and accuse me to these men. Come, inform these men and tell them who it is who improves them. You see, Meletus, that you are silent and know not what to say. Does this not seem shameful to you and a sufficient proof of what I say, that you have not been concerned with any of this? Tell me, my good sir, who improves our young men? — The laws.   e

That is not what I am asking, but what person who has knowledge of the laws to begin with? — These jurymen, Socrates.

How do you mean, Meletus? Are these able to educate the young and improve them? — Certainly.

All of them, or some but not others? — All of them.

Very good, by Hera. You mention a great abundance of benefactors.   25 But what about the audience? Do they improve the young or not? — They do, too.

What about the members of Council?[10] — The Councillors, also.

But, Meletus, what about the assembly? Do members of the assembly corrupt the young, or do they all improve them? — They improve them.

All the Athenians, it seems, make the young into fine good men, except me, and I alone corrupt them. Is that what you mean? — That is most definitely what I mean.

You condemn me to a great misfortune. Tell me: does this also apply   b to horses, do you think? That all men improve them and one individual corrupts them? Or is quite the contrary true, one individual is able to improve them, or very few, namely, the horse breeders, whereas the majority, if they have horses and use them, corrupt them? Is that not the case, Meletus, both with horses and all other animals? Of course

9. Socrates here drops into his usual method of discussion by question and answer. This, no doubt, is what Plato had in mind, at least in part, when he made him ask the indulgence of the jury if he spoke "in his usual manner."

10. The Council was a body of 500 men, elected annually by lot, that prepared the agenda for meetings of the assembly and together with the magistrates conducted the public business of Athens. (On the assembly, see note to *Euthyphro* 3c.)

it is, whether you and Anytus say so or not. It would be a very happy
state of affairs if only one person corrupted our youth, while the others
improved them.

c   You have made it sufficiently obvious, Meletus, that you have never
had any concern for our youth; you show your indifference clearly; that
you have given no thought to the subjects about which you bring me
to trial.

        And by Zeus, Meletus, tell us also whether it is better for a man to
live among good or wicked fellow citizens. Answer, my good man, for
I am not asking a difficult question. Do not the wicked do some harm
to those who are ever closest to them, whereas good people benefit
them? — Certainly.

d   And does the man exist who would rather be harmed than benefited
by his associates? Answer, my good sir, for the law orders you to answer.
Is there any man who wants to be harmed? — Of course not.

        Come now, do you accuse me here of corrupting the young and
making them worse deliberately or unwillingly? — Deliberately.

        What follows, Meletus? Are you so much wiser at your age than I
am at mine that you understand that wicked people always do some
e   harm to their closest neighbors while good people do them good, but
I have reached such a pitch of ignorance that I do not realize this,
namely that if I make one of my associates wicked I run the risk of
being harmed by him so that I do such a great evil deliberately, as you
say? I do not believe you, Meletus, and I do not think anyone else will.
26   Either I do not corrupt the young or, if I do, it is unwillingly, and you
are lying in either case. Now if I corrupt them unwillingly, the law
does not require you to bring people to court for such unwilling wrong-
doings, but to get hold of them privately, to instruct them and exhort
them; for clearly, if I learn better, I shall cease to do what I am doing
unwillingly. You, however, have avoided my company and were unwilling to instruct me, but you bring me here, where the law requires one
to bring those who are in need of punishment, not of instruction.

b   And so, men of Athens, what I said is clearly true: Meletus has never
been at all concerned with these matters. Nonetheless tell us, Meletus,
how you say that I corrupt the young; or is it obvious from your deposition
that it is by teaching them not to believe in the gods in whom the city
believes but in other new spiritual things? Is this not what you say I
teach and so corrupt them? — That is most certainly what I do say.

c   Then by those very gods about whom we are talking, Meletus, make
this clearer to me and to these men: I cannot be sure whether you

mean that I teach the belief that there are some gods—and therefore
I myself believe that there are gods and am not altogether an atheist,
nor am I guilty of that—not, however, the gods in whom the city
believes, but others, and that this is the charge against me, that they
are others. Or whether you mean that I do not believe in gods at all,
and that this is what I teach to others. — This is what I mean, that you
do not believe in gods at all.

You are a strange fellow, Meletus. Why do you say this? Do I not   d
believe, as other men do, that the sun and the moon are gods? — No,
by Zeus, gentlemen of the jury, for he says that the sun is stone, and
the moon earth.

My dear Meletus, do you think you are prosecuting Anaxagoras? Are
you so contemptuous of these men and think them so ignorant of
letters as not to know that the books of Anaxagoras[11] of Clazomenae
are full of those theories, and further, that the young men learn from
me what they can buy from time to time for a drachma, at most, in   e
the bookshops, and ridicule Socrates if he pretends that these theories
are his own, especially as they are so absurd? Is that, by Zeus, what you
think of me, Meletus, that I do not believe that there are any gods?
— That is what I say, that you do not believe in the gods at all.

You cannot be believed, Meletus, even, I think, by yourself. The
man appears to me, men of Athens, highly insolent and uncontrolled.
He seems to have made this deposition out of insolence, violence, and   27
youthful zeal. He is like one who composed a riddle and is trying it
out: "Will the wise Socrates realize that I am jesting and contradicting
myself, or shall I deceive him and others?" I think he contradicts himself
in the affidavit, as if he said: "Socrates is guilty of not believing in gods
but believing in gods," and surely that is the part of a jester!

Examine with me, gentlemen, how he appears to contradict himself,   b
and you, Meletus, answer us. Remember, gentlemen, what I asked
you when I began, not to create a disturbance if I proceed in my
usual manner.

Does any man, Meletus, believe in human activities who does not
believe in humans? Make him answer, and not again and again create

---

11. Anaxagoras of Clazomenae, born about the beginning of the fifth century
B.C., came to Athens as a young man and spent his time in the pursuit of
natural philosophy. He claimed that the universe was directed by Nous (Mind)
and that matter was indestructible but always combining in various ways. He
left Athens after being prosecuted for impiety.

a disturbance. Does any man who does not believe in horses believe
in horsemen's activities? Or in flute-playing activities but not in flute-
players? No, my good sir, no man could. If you are not willing to
answer, I will tell you and these men. Answer the next question, how-

c   ever. Does any man believe in spiritual activities who does not believe
in spirits? — No one.

Thank you for answering, if reluctantly, when these gentlemen made
you. Now you say that I believe in spiritual things and teach about
them, whether new or old, but at any rate spiritual things according to
what you say, and to this you have sworn in your deposition. But if I
believe in spiritual things I must quite inevitably believe in spirits. Is
that not so? It is indeed. I shall assume that you agree, as you do not

d   answer. Do we not believe spirits to be either gods or the children of
gods? Yes or no? — Of course.

Then since I do believe in spirits, as you admit, if spirits are gods,
this is what I mean when I say you speak in riddles and in jest, as you
state that I do not believe in gods and then again that I do, since I do
believe in spirits. If, on the other hand, the spirits are children of the
gods, bastard children of the gods by nymphs or some other mothers,
as they are said to be, what man would believe children of the gods to
exist, but not gods? That would be just as absurd as to believe the young

e   of horses and asses, namely mules, to exist, but not to believe in the
existence of horses and asses. You must have made this deposition,
Meletus, either to test us or because you were at a loss to find any true
wrongdoing of which to accuse me. There is no way in which you
could persuade anyone of even small intelligence that it is possible for
one and the same man to believe in spiritual but not also in divine

28 things, and then again for that same man to believe neither in spirits
nor in gods nor in heroes.

I do not think, men of Athens, that it requires a prolonged defense
to prove that I am not guilty of the charges in Meletus' deposition, but
this is sufficient. On the other hand, you know that what I said earlier
is true, that I am very unpopular with many people. This will be my
undoing, if I am undone, not Meletus or Anytus but the slanders and

b   envy of many people. This has destroyed many other good men and
will, I think, continue to do so. There is no danger that it will stop at me.

Someone might say: "Are you not ashamed, Socrates, to have followed the kind of occupation that has led to your being now in danger
of death?" However, I should be right to reply to him: "You are wrong,
sir, if you think that a man who is any good at all should take into
account the risk of life or death; he should look to this only in his

actions, whether what he does is right or wrong, whether he is acting
like a good or a bad man." According to your view, all the heroes who   c
died at Troy were inferior people, especially the son of Thetis who was
so contemptuous of danger compared with disgrace.[12] When he was
eager to kill Hector, his goddess mother warned him, as I believe, in
some such words as these: "My child, if you avenge the death of your
comrade, Patroclus, and you kill Hector, you will die yourself, for your
death is to follow immediately after Hector's." Hearing this, he despised
death and danger and was much more afraid to live a coward who did   d
not avenge his friends. "Let me die at once," he said, "when once
I have given the wrongdoer his deserts, rather than remain here, a
laughingstock by the curved ships, a burden upon the earth." Do you
think he gave thought to death and danger?

This is the truth of the matter, men of Athens: wherever a man has
taken a position that he believes to be best, or has been placed by his
commander, there he must I think remain and face danger, without a
thought for death or anything else, rather than disgrace. It would have   e
been a dreadful way to behave, men of Athens, if, at Potidaea, Amphipo-
lis, and Delium, I had, at the risk of death, like anyone else, remained
at my post where those you had elected to command had ordered me,
and then, when the god ordered me, as I thought and believed, to live
the life of a philosopher, to examine myself and others, I had abandoned
my post for fear of death or anything else. That would have been a   29
dreadful thing, and then I might truly have justly been brought here
for not believing that there are gods, disobeying the oracle, fearing
death, and thinking I was wise when I was not. To fear death, gentlemen,
is no other than to think oneself wise when one is not, to think one
knows what one does not know. No one knows whether death may not
be the greatest of all blessings for a man, yet men fear it as if they knew
that it is the greatest of evils. And surely it is the most blameworthy   b
ignorance to believe that one knows what one does not know. It is
perhaps on this point and in this respect, gentlemen, that I differ from
the majority of men, and if I were to claim that I am wiser than anyone
in anything, it would be in this, that, as I have no adequate knowledge
of things in the underworld, so I do not think I have. I do know,
however, that it is wicked and shameful to do wrong, to disobey one's
superior, be he god or man. I shall never fear or avoid things of which
I do not know, whether they may not be good rather than things that   c

---

12. The scene between Thetis and Achilles is from the *Iliad* xviii.94 ff.

I know to be bad. Even if you acquitted me now and did not believe Anytus, who said to you that either I should not have been brought here in the first place, or that now I am here, you cannot avoid executing me, for if I should be acquitted, your sons would practice the teachings of Socrates and all be thoroughly corrupted; if you said to me in this regard: "Socrates, we do not believe Anytus now; we acquit you, but only on condition that you spend no more time on this investigation

d   and do not practice philosophy, and if you are caught doing so you will die"; if, as I say, you were to acquit me on those terms, I would say to you: "Men of Athens, I am grateful and I am your friend, but I will obey the god rather than you, and as long as I draw breath and am able, I shall not cease to practice philosophy, to exhort you and in my usual way to point out to any one of you whom I happen to meet: 'Good Sir, you are an Athenian, a citizen of the greatest city with the

e   greatest reputation for both wisdom and power; are you not ashamed of your eagerness to possess as much wealth, reputation, and honors as possible, while you do not care for nor give thought to wisdom or truth, or the best possible state of your soul?' Then, if one of you disputes this and says he does care, I shall not let him go at once or leave him, but I shall question him, examine him, and test him, and if I do not think he has attained the goodness that he says he has, I shall reproach

30   him because he attaches little importance to the most important things and greater importance to inferior things. I shall treat in this way anyone I happen to meet, young and old, citizen and stranger, and more so the citizens because you are more kindred to me. Be sure that this is what the god orders me to do, and I think there is no greater blessing for the city than my service to the god. For I go around doing nothing but persuading both young and old among you not to care for your

b   body or your wealth in preference to or as strongly as for the best possible state of your soul, as I say to you: Wealth does not bring about excellence, but excellence makes wealth and everything else good for men, both individually and collectively."[13]

Now if by saying this I corrupt the young, this advice must be harmful, but if anyone says that I give different advice, he is talking nonsense. On this point I would say to you, men of Athens: "Whether

c   you believe Anytus or not, whether you acquit me or not, do so on the understanding that this is my course of action, even if I am to face

---

13. Alternatively, this sentence could be translated: "Wealth does not bring about excellence, but excellence brings about wealth and all other public and private blessings for men."

death many times." Do not create a disturbance, gentlemen, but abide by my request not to cry out at what I say but to listen, for I think it will be to your advantage to listen, and I am about to say other things at which you will perhaps cry out. By no means do this. Be sure that if you kill the sort of man I say I am, you will not harm me more than yourselves. Neither Meletus nor Anytus can harm me in any way; he could not harm me, for I do not think it is permitted that a better man   d
be harmed by a worse; certainly he might kill me, or perhaps banish or disfranchise me, which he and maybe others think to be great harm, but I do not think so. I think he is doing himself much greater harm doing what he is doing now, attempting to have a man executed unjustly. Indeed, men of Athens, I am far from making a defense now on my own behalf, as might be thought, but on yours, to prevent you from wrongdoing by mistreating the god's gift to you by condemning me;   e
for if you kill me you will not easily find another like me. I was attached to this city by the god—though it seems a ridiculous thing to say—as upon a great and noble horse which was somewhat sluggish because of its size and needed to be stirred up by a kind of gadfly. It is to fulfill some such function that I believe the god has placed me in the city. I never cease to rouse each and every one of you, to persuade and reproach you all day long and everywhere I find myself in your company.   31

Another such man will not easily come to be among you, gentlemen, and if you believe me you will spare me. You might easily be annoyed with me as people are when they are aroused from a doze, and strike out at me; if convinced by Anytus you could easily kill me, and then you could sleep on for the rest of your days, unless the god, in his care for you, sent you someone else. That I am the kind of person to be a gift of the god to the city you might realize from the fact that it does not seem like human nature for me to have neglected all my own affairs   b
and to have tolerated this neglect now for so many years while I was always concerned with you, approaching each one of you like a father or an elder brother to persuade you to care for virtue. Now if I profited from this by charging a fee for my advice, there would be some sense to it, but you can see for yourselves that, for all their shameless accusations, my accusers have not been able in their impudence to bring forward a witness to say that I have ever received a fee or ever asked   c
for one. I, on the other hand, have a convincing witness that I speak the truth, my poverty.

It may seem strange that while I go around and give this advice privately and interfere in private affairs, I do not venture to go to the assembly and there advise the city. You have heard me give the reason

d   for this in many places. I have a divine or spiritual sign which Meletus
has ridiculed in his deposition. This began when I was a child. It is a
voice, and whenever it speaks it turns me away from something I am
about to do, but it never encourages me to do anything. This is what
has prevented me from taking part in public affairs, and I think it was
quite right to prevent me. Be sure, men of Athens, that if I had long
e   ago attempted to take part in politics, I should have died long ago, and
benefited neither you nor myself. Do not be angry with me for speaking
the truth; no man will survive who genuinely opposes you or any
32   other crowd and prevents the occurrence of many unjust and illegal
happenings in the city. A man who really fights for justice must lead
a private, not a public, life if he is to survive for even a short time.

    I shall give you great proofs of this, not words but what you esteem,
deeds. Listen to what happened to me, that you may know that I will
not yield to any man contrary to what is right, for fear of death, even
if I should die at once for not yielding. The things I shall tell you are
commonplace and smack of the lawcourts, but they are true. I have
b   never held any other office in the city, but I served as a member of the
Council, and our tribe Antiochis was presiding at the time when you
wanted to try as a body the ten generals who had failed to pick up the
survivors of the naval battle.[14] This was illegal, as you all recognized
later. I was the only member of the presiding committee to oppose
your doing something contrary to the laws, and I voted against it. The
orators were ready to prosecute me and take me away, and your shouts
were egging them on, but I thought I should run any risk on the side
c   of law and justice rather than join you, for fear of prison or death, when
you were engaged in an unjust course.

    This happened when the city was still a democracy. When the
oligarchy was established, the Thirty[15] summoned me to the Hall, along

---

14. This was the battle of Arginusae (south of Lesbos) in 406 B.C., the last
Athenian victory of the war. A violent storm prevented the Athenian generals
from rescuing their survivors. For this they were tried in Athens and sentenced
to death by the assembly. They were tried in a body, and it is this to which
Socrates objected in the Council's presiding committee which prepared the
business of the assembly. He obstinately persisted in his opposition, in which
he stood alone, and was overruled by the majority. Six generals who were in
Athens were executed.

15. This was the harsh oligarchy that was set up after the final defeat of Athens
by Sparta in the Peloponnesian War in 404 B.C. and that ruled Athens for some
nine months in 404–3 before the democracy was restored.

with four others, and ordered us to bring Leon from Salamis, that he
might be executed. They gave many such orders to many people, in
order to implicate as many as possible in their guilt. Then I showed
again, not in words but in action, that, if it were not rather vulgar to   d
say so, death is something I couldn't care less about, but that my whole
concern is not to do anything unjust or impious. That government,
powerful as it was, did not frighten me into any wrongdoing. When we
left the Hall, the other four went to Salamis and brought in Leon, but
I went home. I might have been put to death for this, had not the
government fallen shortly afterwards. There are many who will witness   e
to these events.

Do you think I would have survived all these years if I were engaged
in public affairs and, acting as a good man must, came to the help of
justice and considered this the most important thing? Far from it, men
of Athens, nor would any other man. Throughout my life, in any public   33
activity I may have engaged in, I am the same man as I am in private
life. I have never come to an agreement with anyone to act unjustly,
neither with anyone else nor with any one of those who they slanderously
say are my pupils. I have never been anyone's teacher. If anyone, young
or old, desires to listen to me when I am talking and dealing with my
own concerns, I have never begrudged this to anyone, but I do not
converse when I receive a fee and not when I do not. I am equally   b
ready to question the rich and the poor if anyone is willing to answer
my questions and listen to what I say. And I cannot justly be held
responsible for the good or bad conduct of these people, as I never
promised to teach them anything and have not done so. If anyone says
that he has learned anything from me, or that he heard anything privately
that the others did not hear, be assured that he is not telling the truth.

Why then do some people enjoy spending considerable time in my   c
company? You have heard why, men of Athens; I have told you the
whole truth. They enjoy hearing those being questioned who think
they are wise, but are not. And this is not unpleasant. To do this has,
as I say, been enjoined upon me by the god, by means of oracles and
dreams, and in every other way that a divine manifestation has ever
ordered a man to do anything. This is true, gentlemen, and can easily
be established.

If I corrupt some young men and have corrupted others, then surely   d
some of them who have grown older and realized that I gave them bad
advice when they were young should now themselves come up here
to accuse me and avenge themselves. If they were unwilling to do so
themselves, then some of their kindred, their fathers or brothers or

other relations should recall it now if their family had been harmed by me. I see many of these present here, first Crito, my contemporary

e and fellow demesman, the father of Critobulus here; next Lysanias of Sphettus, the father of Aeschines here; also Antiphon the Cephisian, the father of Epigenes; and others whose brothers spent their time in this way; Nicostratus, the son of Theozotides, brother of Theodotus, and Theodotus has died so he could not influence him; Paralius here, son of Demodocus, whose brother was Theages; there is Adeimantus,

34 son of Ariston, brother of Plato here; Aeantodorus, brother of Apollodorus here.

I could mention many others, some one of whom surely Meletus should have brought in as witness in his own speech. If he forgot to do so, then let him do it now; I will yield time if he has anything of the kind to say. You will find quite the contrary, gentlemen. These men are all ready to come to the help of the corruptor, the man who

b has harmed their kindred, as Meletus and Anytus say. Now those who were corrupted might well have reason to help me, but the uncorrupted, their kindred who are older men, have no reason to help me except the right and proper one, that they know that Meletus is lying and that I am telling the truth.

Very well, gentlemen. This, and maybe other similar things, is what

c I have to say in my defense. Perhaps one of you might be angry as he recalls that when he himself stood trial on a less dangerous charge, he begged and implored the jurymen with many tears, that he brought his children and many of his friends and family into court to arouse as much pity as he could, but that I do none of these things, even

d though I may seem to be running the ultimate risk. Thinking of this, he might feel resentful towards me and, angry about this, cast his vote in anger. If there is such a one among you—I do not deem there is, but if there is—I think it would be right to say in reply: My good sir, I too have a household and, in Homer's phrase, I am not born "from oak or rock" but from men, so that I have a family, indeed three sons, men of Athens, of whom one is an adolescent while two are children. Nevertheless, I will not beg you to acquit me by bringing them here.

e Why do I do none of these things? Not through arrogance, gentlemen, nor through lack of respect for you. Whether I am brave in the face of death is another matter, but with regard to my reputation and yours and that of the whole city, it does not seem right to me to do these things, especially at my age and with my reputation. For it is generally

35 believed, whether it be true or false, that in certain respects Socrates is

superior to the majority of men. Now if those of you who are considered superior, be it in wisdom or courage or whatever other virtue makes them so, are seen behaving like that, it would be a disgrace. Yet I have often seen them do this sort of thing when standing trial, men who are thought to be somebody, doing amazing things as if they thought it a terrible thing to die, and as if they were to be immortal if you did not execute them. I think these men bring shame upon the city so that a   b
stranger, too, would assume that those who are outstanding in virtue among the Athenians, whom they themselves select from themselves to fill offices of state and receive other honors, are in no way better than women. You should not act like that, men of Athens, those of you who have any reputation at all, and if we do, you should not allow it. You should make it very clear that you will more readily convict a man who performs these pitiful dramatics in court and so makes the city a laughingstock, than a man who keeps quiet.

Quite apart from the question of reputation, gentlemen, I do not think it right to supplicate the jury and to be acquitted because of this,   c
but to teach and persuade them. It is not the purpose of a juryman's office to give justice as a favor to whoever seems good to him, but to judge according to law, and this he has sworn to do. We should not accustom you to perjure yourselves, nor should you make a habit of it. This is irreverent conduct for either of us.

Do not deem it right for me, men of Athens, that I should act towards   d
you in a way that I do not consider to be good or just or pious, especially, by Zeus, as I am being prosecuted by Meletus here for impiety; clearly, if I convinced you by my supplication to do violence to your oath of office, I would be teaching you not to believe that there are gods, and my defense would convict me of not believing in them. This is far from being the case, gentlemen, for I do believe in them as none of my accusers do. I leave it to you and the god to judge me in the way that will be best for me and for you.

[The jury now gives its verdict of guilty, and Meletus asks for the penalty of death.]

There are many other reasons for my not being angry with you for   e
convicting me, men of Athens, and what happened was not unexpected.   36
I am much more surprised at the number of votes cast on each side, for I did not think the decision would be by so few votes but by a great many. As it is, a switch of only thirty votes would have acquitted me. I think myself that I have been cleared of Meletus' charges, and not   b

only this, but it is clear to all that, if Anytus and Lycon had not joined him in accusing me, he would have been fined a thousand drachmas for not receiving a fifth of the votes.

He assesses the penalty at death. So be it. What counter-assessment should I propose to you, men of Athens? Clearly it should be a penalty I deserve, and what do I deserve to suffer or to pay because I have deliberately not led a quiet life but have neglected what occupies most people: wealth, household affairs, the position of general or public orator or the other offices, the political clubs and factions that exist in the city? I thought myself too honest to survive if I occupied myself
c   with those things. I did not follow that path that would have made me of no use either to you or to myself, but I went to each of you privately and conferred upon him what I say is the greatest benefit, by trying to persuade him not to care for any of his belongings before caring that he himself should be as good and as wise as possible, not to care for the city's possessions more than for the city itself, and to care for other
d   things in the same way. What do I deserve for being such a man? Some good, men of Athens, if I must truly make an assessment according to my deserts, and something suitable. What is suitable for a poor benefactor who needs leisure to exhort you? Nothing is more suitable, gentlemen, than for such a man to be fed in the Prytaneum[16]—much more suitable for him than for any one of you who has won a victory at Olympia with a pair or a team of horses. The Olympian victor makes
e   you think yourself happy; I make you be happy. Besides, he does not need food, but I do. So if I must make a just assessment of what I
37 deserve, I assess it as this: free meals in the Prytaneum.

When I say this you may think, as when I spoke of appeals to pity and entreaties, that I speak arrogantly, but that is not the case, men of Athens; rather it is like this: I am convinced that I never willingly wrong anyone, but I am not convincing you of this, for we have talked together
b   but a short time. If it were the law with us, as it is elsewhere, that a trial for life should not last one but many days, you would be convinced, but now it is not easy to dispel great slanders in a short time. Since I am convinced that I wrong no one, I am not likely to wrong myself, to say that I deserve some evil and to make some such assessment against myself. What should I fear? That I should suffer the penalty

16. The Prytaneum was the magistrates' hall or town hall of Athens in which public entertainments were given, particularly to Olympian victors on their return home.

Meletus has assessed against me, of which I say I do not
it is good or bad? Am I then to choose in preference to the
that I know very well to be an evil and assess the penalty at
Imprisonment? Why should I live in prison, always subjected to the
ruling magistrates, the Eleven? A fine, and imprisonment until I pay
it? That would be the same thing for me, as I have no money. Exile?
For perhaps you might accept that assessment.

I should have to be inordinately fond of life, men of Athens, to be
so unreasonable as to suppose that other men will easily tolerate my
company and conversation when you, my fellow citizens, have been   d
unable to endure them, but found them a burden and resented them
so that you are now seeking to get rid of them. Far from it, gentlemen.
It would be a fine life at my age to be driven out of one city after
another, for I know very well that wherever I go the young men will
listen to my talk as they do here. If I drive them away, they will themselves
persuade their elders to drive me out; if I do not drive them away, their   e
fathers and relations will drive me out on their behalf.

Perhaps someone might say: But Socrates, if you leave us will you
not be able to live quietly, without talking? Now this is the most difficult
point on which to convince some of you. If I say that it is impossible   38
for me to keep quiet because that means disobeying the god, you will
not believe me and will think I am being ironical. On the other hand,
if I say that it is the greatest good for a man to discuss virtue every day
and those other things about which you hear me conversing and testing
myself and others, for the unexamined life is not worth living for men,
you will believe me even less.

What I say is true, gentlemen, but it is not easy to convince you. At
the same time, I am not accustomed to think that I deserve any penalty.
If I had money, I would assess the penalty at the amount I could pay,   b
for that would not hurt me, but I have none, unless you are willing to
set the penalty at the amount I can pay, and perhaps I could pay you
one mina of silver. So that is my assessment.

Plato here, men of Athens, and Crito and Critobulus and Apollodorus
bid me put the penalty at thirty minas, and they will stand surety for
the money. Well then, that is my assessment, and they will be sufficient
guarantee of payment.

[The jury now votes again and sentences Socrates to death.]

It is for the sake of a short time, men of Athens, that you will acquire   c
the reputation and the guilt, in the eyes of those who want to denigrate

the city, of having killed Socrates, a wise man, for they who want to revile you will say that I am wise even if I am not. If you had waited but a little while, this would have happened of its own accord. You see

d   my age, that I am already advanced in years and close to death. I am saying this not to all of you but to those who condemned me to death, and to these same ones I say: Perhaps you think that I was convicted for lack of such words as might have convinced you, if I thought I should say or do all I could to avoid my sentence. Far from it. I was convicted because I lacked not words but boldness and shamelessness and the willingness to say to you what you would most gladly have

e   heard from me, lamentations and tears and my saying and doing many things that I say are unworthy of me but that you are accustomed to hear from others. I did not think then that the danger I ran should make me do anything mean, nor do I now regret the nature of my defense. I would much rather die after this kind of defense than live after making the other kind. Neither I nor any other man should, on

39   trial or in war, contrive to avoid death at any cost. Indeed it is often obvious in battle that one could escape death by throwing away one's weapons and by turning to supplicate one's pursuers, and there are many ways to avoid death in every kind of danger if one will venture to do or say anything to avoid it. It is not difficult to avoid death,

b   gentlemen; it is much more difficult to avoid wickedness, for it runs faster than death. Slow and elderly as I am, I have been caught by the slower pursuer, whereas my accusers, being clever and sharp, have been caught by the quicker, wickedness. I leave you now, condemned to death by you, but they are condemned by truth to wickedness and injustice. So I maintain my assessment, and they maintain theirs. This perhaps had to happen, and I think it is as it should be.

c   Now I want to prophesy to those who convicted me, for I am at the point when men prophesy most, when they are about to die. I say, gentlemen, to those who voted to kill me, that vengeance will come upon you immediately after my death, a vengeance much harder to bear than that which you took in killing me. You did this in the belief that you would avoid giving an account of your life, but I maintain that quite the opposite will happen to you. There will be more people

d   to test you, whom I now held back, but you did not notice it. They will be more difficult to deal with as they will be younger and you will resent them more. You are wrong if you believe that by killing people you will prevent anyone from reproaching you for not living in the right way. To escape such tests is neither possible nor good, but it is best and easiest not to discredit others but to prepare oneself to be as good as possible. With this prophecy to you who convicted me, I part from you.

I should be glad to discuss what has happened with those who voted   e
for my acquittal during the time that the officers of the court are busy and I do not yet have to depart to my death. So, gentlemen, stay with me awhile, for nothing prevents us from talking to each other while it is allowed. To you, as being my friends, I want to show the meaning   40
of what has occurred. A surprising thing has happened to me, jurymen—you I would rightly call jurymen. At all previous times my familiar prophetic power, my spiritual manifestation, frequently opposed me, even in small matters, when I was about to do something wrong, but now that, as you can see for yourselves, I was faced with what one might think, and what is generally thought to be, the worst of evils, my divine sign has not opposed me, either when I left home at dawn, or   b
when I came into court, or at any time that I was about to say something during my speech. Yet in other talks it often held me back in the middle of my speaking, but now it has opposed no word or deed of mine. What do I think is the reason for this? I will tell you. What has happened to me may well be a good thing, and those of us who believe death to be an evil are certainly mistaken. I have convincing proof of this, for it is   c
impossible that my familiar sign did not oppose me if I was not about to do what was right.

Let us reflect in this way, too, that there is good hope that death is a blessing, for it is one of two things: either the dead are nothing and have no perception of anything, or it is, as we are told, a change and a relocating for the soul from here to another place. If it is complete   d
lack of perception, like a dreamless sleep, then death would be a great advantage. For I think that if one had to pick out that night during which a man slept soundly and did not dream, put beside it the other nights and days of his life, and then see how many days and nights had been better and more pleasant than that night, not only a private person but the great king would find them easy to count compared with the   e
other days and nights. If death is like this I say it is an advantage, for all eternity would then seem to be no more than a single night. If, on the other hand, death is a change from here to another place, and what we are told is true and all who have died are there, what greater blessing could there be, gentlemen of the jury? If anyone arriving in Hades will   41
have escaped from those who call themselves jurymen here, and will find those true jurymen who are said to sit in judgment there, Minos

and Rhadamanthus and Aeacus and Triptolemus and the other demi-
gods who have been upright in their own life, would that be a poor
kind of change? Again, what would one of you give to keep company
with Orpheus and Musaeus, Hesiod and Homer? I am willing to die
many times if that is true. It would be a wonderful way for me to spend

b my time whenever I met Palamedes and Ajax, the son of Telamon,
and any other of the men of old who died through an unjust conviction,
to compare my experience with theirs. I think it would be pleasant.
Most important, I could spend my time testing and examining people
there, as I do here, as to who among them is wise, and who thinks he
is, but is not.

What would one not give, gentlemen of the jury, for the opportunity

c to examine the man who led the great expedition against Troy, or
Odysseus, or Sisyphus, and innumerable other men and women one
could mention? It would be an extraordinary happiness to talk with
them, to keep company with them and examine them. In any case,
they would certainly not put one to death for doing so. They are happier
there than we are here in other respects, and for the rest of time they
are deathless, if indeed what we are told is true.

You too must be of good hope as regards death, gentlemen of the
jury, and keep this one truth in mind, that a good man cannot be

d harmed either in life or in death, and that his affairs are not neglected
by the gods. What has happened to me now has not happened of itself,
but it is clear to me that it was better for me to die now and to escape
from trouble. That is why my divine sign did not oppose me at any
point. So I am certainly not angry with those who convicted me, or
with my accusers. Of course that was not their purpose when they
accused and convicted me, but they thought they were hurting me,

e and for this they deserve blame. This much I ask from them: When
my sons grow up, avenge yourselves by causing them the same kind of
grief that I caused you, if you think they care for money or anything
else more than they care for virtue, or if they think they are somebody
when they are nobody. Reproach them as I reproach you, that they do
not care for the right things and think they are worthy when they are

42 not worthy of anything. If you do this, I shall have been justly treated
by you, and my sons also.

Now the hour to part has come. I go to die, you go to live. Which
of us goes to the better lot is known to no one, except the god.

CRITO

*About the time of Socrates' trial, a state galley had set out on an
annual religious mission to the small Aegean island of Delos, sacred
to Apollo, and while it was away, no execution was allowed to take
place. So it was that Socrates was kept in prison for a month after the
trial. The ship has now arrived at Cape Sunium in Attica and is thus
expected at the Piraeus, Athens' port, momentarily. So Socrates' old
and faithful friend, Crito, makes one last effort to persuade him to
escape into exile, and all arrangements for this plan have been made.
It is this conversation between the two old friends that Plato professes
to report in this dialogue. It is, as Crito plainly tells him, his last
chance, but Socrates will not take it, and he gives his reasons for his
refusal. Whether this conversation took place at this particular time is
not important, for there is every reason to believe that Socrates' friends
tried to plan his escape and that he refused. Plato more than hints
that the authorities would not have minded much, as long as he left
the country.*

G.M.A.G.

SOCRATES: Why have you come so early, Crito? Or is it not still early? 43

CRITO: It certainly is.

SOCRATES: How early?

CRITO: Early dawn.

SOCRATES: I am surprised that the warder was willing to listen to you.

CRITO: He is quite friendly to me by now, Socrates. I have been
here often and I have given him something.

SOCRATES: Have you just come, or have you been here for some time?

CRITO: A fair time.

SOCRATES: Then why did you not wake me right away but sit there b
in silence?

CRITO: By Zeus no, Socrates. I would not myself want to be in
distress and awake so long. I have been surprised to see you so peacefully
asleep. It was on purpose that I did not wake you, so that you should

spend your time most agreeably. Often in the past throughout my life, I have considered the way you live happy, and especially so now that you bear your present misfortune so easily and lightly.

SOCRATES: It would not be fitting at my age to resent the fact that I must die now.

c   CRITO: Other men of your age are caught in such misfortunes, but their age does not prevent them resenting their fate.

SOCRATES: That is so. Why have you come so early?

CRITO: I bring bad news, Socrates, not for you, apparently, but for me and all your friends the news is bad and hard to bear. Indeed, I would count it among the hardest.

SOCRATES: What is it? Or has the ship arrived from Delos, at the
d   arrival of which I must die?

CRITO: It has not arrived yet, but it will, I believe, arrive today, according to a message some men brought from Sunium, where they left it. This makes it obvious that it will come today, and that your life must end tomorrow.

SOCRATES: May it be for the best. If it so please the gods, so be it. However, I do not think it will arrive today.

44   CRITO: What indication have you of this?

SOCRATES: I will tell you. I must die the day after the ship arrives.

CRITO: That is what those in authority say.

SOCRATES: Then I do not think it will arrive on this coming day, but on the next. I take to witness of this a dream I had a little earlier during this night. It looks as if it was the right time for you not to wake me.

CRITO: What was your dream?

SOCRATES: I thought that a beautiful and comely woman dressed in white approached me. She called me and said: "Socrates, may you
b   arrive at fertile Phthia[1] on the third day."

CRITO: A strange dream, Socrates.

---

1. A quotation from the ninth book of the *Iliad* (363). Achilles has rejected all the presents of Agamemnon for him to return to the battle and threatens to go home. He says his ships will sail in the morning, and with good weather he might arrive on the third day "in fertile Phthia" (which is his home). Socrates takes the dream to mean that he will die, and his soul will find its home, on the third day. As always, counting the first member of a series, the third day is the day after tomorrow.

SOCRATES: But it seems clear enough to me, Crito.

CRITO: Too clear it seems, my dear Socrates, but listen to me even now and be saved. If you die, it will not be a single misfortune for me. Not only will I be deprived of a friend, the like of whom I shall never find again, but many people who do not know you or me very well will think that I could have saved you if I were willing to spend money,   c but that I did not care to do so. Surely there can be no worse reputation than to be thought to value money more highly than one's friends, for the majority will not believe that you yourself were not willing to leave prison while we were eager for you to do so.

SOCRATES: My good Crito, why should we care so much for what the majority think? The most reasonable people, to whom one should pay more attention, will believe that things were done as they were done.

CRITO: You see, Socrates, that one must also pay attention to the   d opinion of the majority. Your present situation makes clear that the majority can inflict not the least but pretty well the greatest evils if one is slandered among them.

SOCRATES: Would that the majority could inflict the greatest evils, for they would then be capable of the greatest good, and that would be fine, but now they cannot do either. They cannot make a man either wise or foolish, but they inflict things haphazardly.

CRITO: That may be so. But tell me this, Socrates, are you anticipating   e that I and your other friends would have trouble with the informers if you escape from here, as having stolen you away, and that we should be compelled to lose all our property or pay heavy fines and suffer other punishment besides? If you have any such fear, forget it. We would be   45 justified in running this risk to save you, and worse, if necessary. Do follow my advice, and do not act differently.

SOCRATES: I do have these things in mind, Crito, and also many others.

CRITO: Have no such fear. It is not much money that some people require to save you and get you out of here. Further, do you not see that those informers are cheap, and that not much money would be needed to deal with them? My money is available and is, I think,   b sufficient. If, because of your affection for me, you feel you should not spend any of mine, there are those strangers here ready to spend money. One of them, Simmias the Theban, has brought enough for this very purpose. Cebes, too, and a good many others. So, as I say, do not let this fear make you hesitate to save yourself, nor let what you said in

court trouble you, that you would not know what to do with yourself
c   if you left Athens, for you would be welcomed in many places to which
you might go. If you want to go to Thessaly, I have friends there who
will greatly appreciate you and keep you safe, so that no one in Thessaly
will harm you.

Besides, Socrates, I do not think that what you are doing is just, to
give up your life when you can save it, and to hasten your fate as your
enemies would hasten it, and indeed have hastened it in their wish to
destroy you. Moreover, I think you are betraying your sons by going
d   away and leaving them, when you could bring them up and educate
them. You thus show no concern for what their fate may be. They will
probably have the usual fate of orphans. Either one should not have
children, or one should share with them to the end the toil of upbringing
and education. You seem to me to choose the easiest path, whereas
one should choose the path a good and courageous man would choose,
particularly when one claims throughout one's life to care for virtue.

e   I feel ashamed on your behalf and on behalf of us, your friends, lest
all that has happened to you be thought due to cowardice on our part:
the fact that your trial came to court when it need not have done so,
the handling of the trial itself, and now this absurd ending which will
be thought to have got beyond our control through some cowardice
46 and unmanliness on our part, since we did not save you, or you save
yourself, when it was possible and could be done if we had been of
the slightest use. Consider, Socrates, whether this is not only evil, but
shameful, both for you and for us. Take counsel with yourself, or rather
the time for counsel is past and the decision should have been taken,
and there is no further opportunity, for this whole business must be
ended tonight. If we delay now, then it will no longer be possible; it
will be too late. Let me persuade you on every count, Socrates, and do
not act otherwise.

b   SOCRATES: My dear Crito, your eagerness is worth much if it should
have some right aim; if not, then the greater your keenness the more
difficult it is to deal with. We must therefore examine whether we
should act in this way or not, as not only now but at all times I am the
kind of man who listens to nothing within me but the argument that
on reflection seems best to me. I cannot, now that this fate has come
c   upon me, discard the arguments I used; they seem to me much the
same. I value and respect the same principles as before, and if we have
no better arguments to bring up at this moment, be sure that I shall
not agree with you, not even if the power of the majority were to

frighten us with more bogeys, as if we were children, with threats of incarcerations and executions and confiscation of property. How should we examine this matter most reasonably? Would it be by taking up first your argument about the opinions of men, whether it is sound in every   d
case that one should pay attention to some opinions, but not to others? Or was that well-spoken before the necessity to die came upon me, but now it is clear that this was said in vain for the sake of argument, that it was in truth play and nonsense? I am eager to examine together with you, Crito, whether this argument will appear in any way different to me in my present circumstances, or whether it remains the same, whether we are to abandon it or believe it. It was said on every occasion by those who thought they were speaking sensibly, as I have just now   e
been speaking, that one should greatly value some people's opinions, but not others. Does that seem to you a sound statement?

You, as far as a human being can tell, are exempt from the likelihood of dying tomorrow, so the present misfortune is not likely to lead you   47
astray. Consider then, do you not think it a sound statement that one must not value all the opinions of men, but some and not others, nor the opinions of all men, but those of some and not of others? What do you say? Is this not well said?

CRITO: It is.

SOCRATES: One should value the good opinions, and not the bad ones?

CRITO: Yes.

SOCRATES: The good opinions are those of wise men, the bad ones those of foolish men?

CRITO: Of course.

SOCRATES: Come then, what of statements such as this: Should a man professionally engaged in physical training pay attention to the   b
praise and blame and opinion of any man, or to those of one man only, namely a doctor or trainer?

CRITO: To those of one only.

SOCRATES: He should therefore fear the blame and welcome the praise of that one man, and not those of the many?

CRITO: Obviously.

SOCRATES: He must then act and exercise, eat and drink in the way the one, the trainer and the one who knows, thinks right, not all the others?

CRITO: That is so.

c   SOCRATES: Very well. And if he disobeys the one, disregards his opinion and his praises while valuing those of the many who have no knowledge, will he not suffer harm?

CRITO: Of course.

SOCRATES: What is that harm, where does it tend, and what part of the man who disobeys does it affect?

CRITO: Obviously the harm is to his body, which it ruins.

SOCRATES: Well said. So with other matters, not to enumerate them all, and certainly with actions just and unjust, shameful and beautiful, good and bad, about which we are now deliberating, should we follow
d   the opinion of the many and fear it, or that of the one, if there is one who has knowledge of these things and before whom we feel fear and shame more than before all the others? If we do not follow his directions, we shall harm and corrupt that part of ourselves that is improved by just actions and destroyed by unjust actions. Or is there nothing in this?

CRITO: I think there certainly is, Socrates.

SOCRATES: Come now, if we ruin that which is improved by health and corrupted by disease by not following the opinions of those who
e   know, is life worth living for us when that is ruined? And that is the body, is it not?

CRITO: Yes.

SOCRATES: And is life worth living with a body that is corrupted and in bad condition?

CRITO: In no way.

SOCRATES: And is life worth living for us with that part of us corrupted that unjust action harms and just action benefits? Or do we think that part of us, whatever it is, that is concerned with justice and injustice,
48   is inferior to the body?

CRITO: Not at all.

SOCRATES: It is more valuable?

CRITO: Much more.

SOCRATES: We should not then think so much of what the majority will say about us, but what he will say who understands justice and injustice, the one, that is, and the truth itself. So that, in the first place, you were wrong to believe that we should care for the opinion of the many about what is just, beautiful, good, and their opposites. "But," someone might say, "the many are able to put us to death."

CRITO: That too is obvious, Socrates, and someone might well say so.   b

SOCRATES: And, my admirable friend, that argument that we have gone through remains, I think, as before. Examine the following statement in turn as to whether it stays the same or not, that the most important thing is not life, but the good life.

CRITO: It stays the same.

SOCRATES: And that the good life, the beautiful life, and the just life are the same; does that still hold, or not?

CRITO: It does hold.

SOCRATES: As we have agreed so far, we must examine next whether it is just for me to try to get out of here when the Athenians have not acquitted me. If it is seen to be just, we will try to do so; if it is not,   c we will abandon the idea. As for those questions you raise about money, reputation, the upbringing of children, Crito, those considerations in truth belong to those people who easily put men to death and would bring them to life again if they could, without thinking; I mean the majority of men. For us, however, since our argument leads to this, the only valid consideration, as we were saying just now, is whether we should be acting rightly in giving money and gratitude to those who   d will lead me out of here, and ourselves helping with the escape, or whether in truth we shall do wrong in doing all this. If it appears that we shall be acting unjustly, then we have no need at all to take into account whether we shall have to die if we stay here and keep quiet, or suffer in another way, rather than do wrong.

CRITO: I think you put that beautifully, Socrates, but see what we should do.

SOCRATES: Let us examine the question together, my dear friend,   e and if you can make any objection while I am speaking, make it and I will listen to you, but if you have no objection to make, my dear Crito, then stop now from saying the same thing so often, that I must leave here against the will of the Athenians. I think it important to persuade you before I act, and not to act against your wishes. See whether the start of our inquiry is adequately stated, and try to answer   49 what I ask you in the way you think best.

CRITO: I shall try.

SOCRATES: Do we say that one must never in any way do wrong willingly, or must one do wrong in one way and not in another? Is to do wrong never good or admirable, as we have agreed in the past, or have all these former agreements been washed out during the last few
b   days? Have we at our age failed to notice for some time that in our serious discussions we were no different from children? Above all, is the truth such as we used to say it was, whether the majority agree or not, and whether we must still suffer worse things than we do now, or will be treated more gently, that, nonetheless, wrongdoing or injustice is in every way harmful and shameful to the wrongdoer? Do we say so or not?

CRITO: We do.

SOCRATES: So one must never do wrong.

CRITO: Certainly not.

SOCRATES: Nor must one, when wronged, inflict wrong in return, as the majority believe, since one must never do wrong.

c   CRITO: That seems to be the case.

SOCRATES: Come now, should one do harm to anyone or not, Crito?

CRITO: One must never do so.

SOCRATES: Well then, if one is oneself done harm, is it right, as the majority say, to do harm in return, or is it not?

CRITO: It is never right.

SOCRATES: Doing people harm is no different from wrongdoing.

CRITO: That is true.

SOCRATES: One should never do wrong in return, nor do any man harm, no matter what he may have done to you. And Crito, see that
d   you do not agree to this, contrary to your belief. For I know that only a few people hold this view or will hold it, and there is no common ground between those who hold this view and those who do not, but they inevitably despise each other's views. So then consider very carefully whether we have this view in common, and whether you agree, and let this be the basis of our deliberation, that neither to do wrong nor to return a wrong is ever correct, nor is doing harm in return for harm done. Or do you disagree and do not share this view as a basis
e   for discussion? I have held it for a long time and still hold it now, but if you think otherwise, tell me now. If, however, you stick to our former opinion, then listen to the next point.

CRITO: I stick to it and agree with you. So say on.

SOCRATES: Then I state the next point, or rather I ask you: when one has come to an agreement that is just with someone, should one fulfill it or cheat on it?

CRITO: One should fulfill it.

SOCRATES: See what follows from this: if we leave here without the city's permission, are we harming people whom we should least do   50 harm to? And are we sticking to a just agreement, or not?

CRITO: I cannot answer your question, Socrates. I do not know.

SOCRATES: Look at it this way. If, as we were planning to run away from here, or whatever one should call it, the laws and the state came and confronted us and asked: "Tell me, Socrates, what are you intending to do? Do you not by this action you are attempting intend to destroy us, the laws, and indeed the whole city, as far as you are concerned?   b Or do you think it possible for a city not to be destroyed if the verdicts of its courts have no force but are nullified and set at naught by private individuals?" What shall we answer to this and other such arguments? For many things could be said, especially by an orator on behalf of this law we are destroying, which orders that the judgments of the courts shall be carried out. Shall we say in answer, "The city wronged me,   c and its decision was not right." Shall we say that, or what?

CRITO: Yes, by Zeus, Socrates, that is our answer.

SOCRATES: Then what if the laws said: "Was that the agreement between us, Socrates, or was it to respect the judgments that the city came to?" And if we wondered at their words, they would perhaps add: "Socrates, do not wonder at what we say but answer, since you are accustomed to proceed by question and answer. Come now, what accusation do you bring against us and the city, that you should try to   d destroy us? Did we not, first, bring you to birth, and was it not through us that your father married your mother and begat you? Tell us, do you find anything to criticize in those of us who are concerned with marriage?" And I would say that I do not criticize them. "Or in those of us concerned with the nurture of babies and the education that you too received? Were those assigned to that subject not right to instruct your father to educate you in the arts and in physical culture?" And I   e would say that they were right. "Very well," they would continue, "and after you were born and nurtured and educated, could you, in the first place, deny that you are our offspring and servant, both you and your forefathers? If that is so, do you think that we are on an equal footing

as regards the right, and that whatever we do to you it is right for you
to do to us? You were not on an equal footing with your father as
regards the right, nor with your master if you had one, so as to retaliate
51 for anything they did to you, to revile them if they reviled you, to beat
them if they beat you, and so with many other things. Do you think
you have this right to retaliation against your country and its laws? That
if we undertake to destroy you and think it right to do so, you can
undertake to destroy us, as far as you can, in return? And will you say
that you are right to do so, you who truly care for virtue? Is your wisdom
such as not to realize that your country is to be honored more than
your mother, your father, and all your ancestors, that it is more to be
b revered and more sacred, and that it counts for more among the gods
and sensible men, that you must worship it, yield to it, and placate its
anger more than your father's? You must either persuade it or obey its
orders, and endure in silence whatever it instructs you to endure,
whether blows or bonds, and if it leads you into war to be wounded or
killed, you must obey. To do so is right, and one must not give way or
retreat or leave one's post, but both in war and in courts and everywhere
c else, one must obey the commands of one's city and country, or persuade
it as to the nature of justice. It is impious to bring violence to bear
against your mother or father; it is much more so to use it against your
country." What shall we say in reply, Crito, that the laws speak the
truth, or not?

CRITO: I think they do.

SOCRATES: "Reflect now, Socrates," the laws might say, "that if what
we say is true, you are not treating us rightly by planning to do what
you are planning. We have given you birth, nurtured you, educated
d you; we have given you and all other citizens a share of all the good
things we could. Even so, by giving every Athenian the opportunity,
once arrived at voting age and having observed the affairs of the city
and us the laws, we proclaim that if we do not please him, he can take
his possessions and go wherever he pleases. Not one of our laws raises
any obstacle or forbids him, if he is not satisfied with us or the city, if
one of you wants to go and live in a colony or wants to go anywhere
e else, and keep his property. We say, however, that whoever of you
remains, when he sees how we conduct our trials and manage the city
in other ways, has in fact come to an agreement with us to obey our
instructions. We say that the one who disobeys does wrong in three
ways, first because in us he disobeys his parents, also those who brought
him up, and because, in spite of his agreement, he neither obeys us

nor, if we do something wrong, does he try to persuade us to do better. Yet we only propose things, we do not issue savage commands to do whatever we order; we give two alternatives, either to persuade us or to do what we say. He does neither. We do say that you too, Socrates, are open to those charges if you do what you have in mind; you would be among, not the least, but the most guilty of the Athenians." And if I should say "Why so?" they might well be right to upbraid me and say that I am among the Athenians who most definitely came to that agreement with them. They might well say: "Socrates, we have convincing proofs that we and the city were congenial to you. You would not have dwelt here most consistently of all the Athenians if the city had not been exceedingly pleasing to you. You have never left the city, even to see a festival, nor for any other reason except military service; you have never gone to stay in any other city, as people do; you have had no desire to know another city or other laws; we and our city satisfied you.

"So decisively did you choose us and agree to be a citizen under us. Also, you have had children in this city, thus showing that it was congenial to you. Then at your trial you could have assessed your penalty at exile if you wished, and you are now attempting to do against the city's wishes what you could then have done with her consent. Then you prided yourself that you did not resent death, but you chose, as you said, death in preference to exile. Now, however, those words do not make you ashamed, and you pay no heed to us, the laws, as you plan to destroy us, and you act like the meanest type of slave by trying to run away, contrary to your commitments and your agreement to live as a citizen under us. First then, answer us on this very point, whether we speak the truth when we say that you agreed, not only in words but by your deeds, to live in accordance with us." What are we to say to that, Crito? Must we not agree?

CRITO: We must, Socrates.

SOCRATES: "Surely," they might say, "you are breaking the commitments and agreements that you made with us without compulsion or deceit, and under no pressure of time for deliberation. You have had seventy years during which you could have gone away if you did not like us, and if you thought our agreements unjust. You did not choose to go to Sparta or to Crete, which you are always saying are well governed, nor to any other city, Greek or foreign. You have been away from Athens less than the lame or the blind or other handicapped people. It is clear that the city has been outstandingly more congenial to you than to other Athenians, and so have we, the laws, for what city can please without laws? Will you then not now stick to our agreements? You will, Socrates, if we can persuade you, and not make yourself a laughingstock by leaving the city.

"For consider what good you will do yourself or your friends by breaking our agreements and committing such a wrong. It is pretty obvious that your friends will themselves be in danger of exile, disfran-
b   chisement, and loss of property. As for yourself, if you go to one of the nearby cities—Thebes or Megara, both are well governed—you will arrive as an enemy to their government; all who care for their city will look on you with suspicion, as a destroyer of the laws. You will also strengthen the conviction of the jury that they passed the right sentence
c   on you, for anyone who destroys the laws could easily be thought to corrupt the young and the ignorant. Or will you avoid cities that are well governed and men who are civilized? If you do this, will your life be worth living? Will you have social intercourse with them and not be ashamed to talk to them? And what will you say? The same as you did here, that virtue and justice are man's most precious possession,
d   along with lawful behavior and the laws? Do you not think that Socrates would appear to be an unseemly kind of person? One must think so. Or will you leave those places and go to Crito's friends in Thessaly? There you will find the greatest license and disorder, and they may enjoy hearing from you how absurdly you escaped from prison in some disguise, in a leather jerkin or some other things in which escapees wrap themselves, thus altering your appearance. Will there be no one to say that you, likely to live but a short time more, were so greedy for
e   life that you transgressed the most important laws? Possibly, Socrates, if you do not annoy anyone, but if you do, many disgraceful things will be said about you.

"You will spend your time ingratiating yourself with all men, and be at their beck and call. What will you do in Thessaly but feast, as if you had gone to a banquet in Thessaly? As for those conversations of yours
54   about justice and the rest of virtue, where will they be? You say you want to live for the sake of your children, that you may bring them up and educate them. How so? Will you bring them up and educate them by taking them to Thessaly and making strangers of them, that they may enjoy that too? Or not so, but they will be better brought up and educated here, while you are alive, though absent? Yes, your friends will look after them. Will they look after them if you go and live in Thessaly, but not if you go away to the underworld? If those who profess themselves your
b   friends are any good at all, one must assume that they will.

"Be persuaded by us who have brought you up, Socrates. Do not value either your children or your life or anything else more than goodness, in order that when you arrive in Hades you may have all this as your defense before the rulers there. If you do this deed, you will not think it better or more just or more pious here, nor will any one of your friends, nor will it be better for you when you arrive yonder. As it is, you depart, if you depart, after being wronged not by us, the laws, but by men; but if you depart after shamefully returning wrong c for wrong and mistreatment for mistreatment, after breaking your agreements and commitments with us, after mistreating those you should mistreat least—yourself, your friends, your country, and us—we shall be angry with you while you are still alive, and our brothers, the laws of the underworld, will not receive you kindly, knowing that you tried to destroy us as far as you could. Do not let Crito persuade you, rather than us, to do what he says."   d

Crito, my dear friend, be assured that these are the words I seem to hear, as the Corybants seem to hear the music of their flutes, and the echo of these words resounds in me, and makes it impossible for me to hear anything else. As far as my present beliefs go, if you speak in opposition to them, you will speak in vain. However, if you think you can accomplish anything, speak.

CRITO: I have nothing to say, Socrates.

SOCRATES: Let it be then, Crito, and let us act in this way, since e this is the way the god is leading us.

MENO

Meno's is one of the leading aristocratic families of Thessaly—whose capital was Larissa—traditionally friendly to Athens and Athenian interests. Here he is a young man, about to embark on an unscrupulous military and political career, leading to an early death at the hands of the Persian king. To his aristocratic "virtue" (Plato's ancient readers would know what that ultimately came to) he adds an admiration for ideas on the subject he has learned from the rhetorician Gorgias (about whom we learn more in the dialogue named after him). What brings Meno to Athens we are not told. His family's local sponsor is the democratic politician Anytus, one of Socrates' accusers at his trial, and apparently Anytus is Meno's host. The dialogue begins abruptly, without stage-setting preliminaries of the sort we find in the "Socratic" dialogues, and with no context of any kind being provided for the conversation. Meno wants to know Socrates' position on the then much-debated question whether virtue can be taught, or whether it comes rather by practice, or else is acquired by one's birth and nature, or in some other way. Socrates and Meno pursue that question, and the preliminary one of what virtue indeed is, straight through to the inconclusive conclusion characteristic of "Socratic" dialogues. (Anytus joins the conversation briefly. He bristles when, to support his doubts that virtue can be taught, Socrates points to the failure of famous Athenian leaders to pass their own virtue on to their sons, and he issues a veiled threat of the likely consequences to Socrates of such "slanderous" attacks.)

The dialogue is best remembered, however, for the interlude in which Socrates questions Meno's slave about a problem in geometry— how to find a square double in area to any given square. Having determined that Meno does not know what virtue is, and recognizing that he himself does not know either, Socrates has proposed to Meno that they inquire into this together. Meno protests that that is impossible, challenging Socrates with the "paradox" that one logically cannot inquire productively into what one does not already know—nor of course into what one already does! Guided by Socrates' questions, the slave (who has never studied geometry before) comes to see for himself, to recognize, what the right answer to the geometrical problem

must be. Socrates argues that this confirms something he has heard
from certain wise priests and priestesses—that the soul is immortal and
that at our birth we already possess all theoretical knowledge (he
includes here not just mathematical theory but moral knowledge as
well). Prodded by Socrates' questions, the slave was "recollecting" this
prior knowledge, not drawing new conclusions from data being
presented to him for the first time. So in moral inquiry, as well, there
is hope that, if we question ourselves rightly, "recollection" can
progressively improve our understanding of moral truth and eventually
lead us to full knowledge of it.

The examination of the slave assuages Meno's doubt about the
possibility of such inquiry. He and Socrates proceed to inquire together
what virtue is—but now they follow a new method of "hypothesis"
introduced by Socrates again by analogy with procedures in geometry.
Socrates no longer asks Meno for his views and criticizes those. Among
other "hypotheses" that he now works with, he advances and argues for
a hypothesis of his own, that virtue is knowledge (in which case it
must be teachable). But he also considers weaknesses in his own
argument, leading to the alternative possible hypothesis, that virtue is
god-granted right opinion (and so, not teachable). In the second half
of the dialogue we thus see a new Socrates, with new methods of
argument and inquiry, not envisioned in such "Socratic" dialogues as
Euthyphro, Laches, and Charmides. Meno points forward to Phaedo,
where the thesis that theoretical knowledge comes by recollection is
discussed again, with a clear reference back to Meno, but now
expanded by the addition of Platonic Forms as objects of recollection
and knowledge.

                                                        J.M.C.

MENO: Can you tell me, Socrates, can virtue be taught? Or is it not   70
teachable but the result of practice, or is it neither of these, but men
possess it by nature or in some other way?

SOCRATES: Before now, Meno, Thessalians had a high reputation
among the Greeks and were admired for their horsemanship and their
wealth, but now, it seems to me, they are also admired for their wisdom,   b
not least the fellow citizens of your friend Aristippus of Larissa. The
responsibility for this reputation of yours lies with Gorgias, for when
he came to your city he found that the leading Aleuadae, your lover

Aristippus among them, loved him for his wisdom, and so did the other leading Thessalians. In particular, he accustomed you to give a bold and grand answer to any question you may be asked, as experts are

c likely to do. Indeed, he himself was ready to answer any Greek who wished to question him, and every question was answered. But here in Athens, my dear Meno, the opposite is the case, as if there were a dearth of wisdom, and wisdom seems to have departed hence to go to

71 you. If then you want to ask one of us that sort of question, everyone will laugh and say: "Good stranger, you must think me happy indeed if you think I know whether virtue can be taught or how it comes to be; I am so far from knowing whether virtue can be taught or not that I do not even have any knowledge of what virtue itself is."

b I myself, Meno, am as poor as my fellow citizens in this matter, and I blame myself for my complete ignorance about virtue. If I do not know what something is, how could I know what qualities it possesses? Or do you think that someone who does not know at all who Meno is could know whether he is good-looking or rich or well-born, or the opposite of these? Do you think that is possible?

MENO: I do not; but, Socrates, do you really not know what virtue

c is? Are we to report this to the folk back home about you?

SOCRATES: Not only that, my friend, but also that, as I believe, I have never yet met anyone else who did know.

MENO: How so? Did you not meet Gorgias when he was here?

SOCRATES: I did.

MENO: Did you then not think that he knew?

SOCRATES: I do not altogether remember, Meno, so that I cannot tell you now what I thought then. Perhaps he does know; you know

d what he used to say, so you remind me of what he said. You tell me yourself, if you are willing, for surely you share his views. — I do.

SOCRATES: Let us leave Gorgias out of it, since he is not here. But Meno, by the gods, what do you yourself say that virtue is? Speak and do not begrudge us, so that I may have spoken a most unfortunate untruth when I said that I had never met anyone who knew, if you and Gorgias are shown to know.

e MENO: It is not hard to tell you, Socrates. First, if you want the virtue of a man, it is easy to say that a man's virtue consists of being able to manage public affairs and in so doing to benefit his friends and harm his enemies and to be careful that no harm comes to himself; if you want the virtue of a woman, it is not difficult to describe: she must manage the home well, preserve its possessions, and be submissive to her husband; the virtue of a child, whether male or female, is different again, and so is that of an elderly man, if you want that, or if you want that of a free man or a slave. And there are very many other virtues, so   72 that one is not at a loss to say what virtue is. There is virtue for every action and every age, for every task of ours and every one of us—and, Socrates, the same is true for wickedness.

SOCRATES: I seem to be in great luck, Meno; while I am looking for one virtue, I have found you to have a whole swarm of them. But, Meno, to follow up the image of swarms, if I were asking you what is   b the nature of bees, and you said that they are many and of all kinds, what would you answer if I asked you: "Do you mean that they are many and varied and different from one another insofar as they are bees? Or are they no different in that regard, but in some other respect, in their beauty, for example, or their size or in some other such way?" Tell me, what would you answer if thus questioned?

MENO: I would say that they do not differ from one another in being bees.

SOCRATES: If I went on to say: "Tell me, what is this very thing, Meno, in which they are all the same and do not differ from one   c another?" Would you be able to tell me?

MENO: I would.

SOCRATES: The same is true in the case of the virtues. Even if they are many and various, all of them have one and the same form which makes them virtues, and it is right to look to this when one is asked to make clear what virtue is. Or do you not understand what I mean?   d

MENO: I think I understand, but I certainly do not grasp the meaning of the question as fully as I want to.

SOCRATES: I am asking whether you think it is only in the case of virtue that there is one for man, another for woman, and so on, or is the same true in the case of health and size and strength? Do you think that there is one health for man and another for woman? Or, if it is health, does it have the same form everywhere, whether in man or in   e anything else whatever?

MENO: The health of a man seems to me the same as that of a woman.

SOCRATES: And so with size and strength? If a woman is strong, that strength will be the same and have the same form, for by "the same"

I mean that strength is no different as far as being strength, whether in a man or a woman. Or do you think there is a difference?

MENO: I do not think so.

SOCRATES: And will there be any difference in the case of virtue, as
73 far as being virtue is concerned, whether it be in a child or an old man, in a woman or in a man?

MENO: I think, Socrates, that somehow this is no longer like those other cases.

SOCRATES: How so? Did you not say that the virtue of a man consists of managing the city well, and that of a woman of managing the household? — I did.

SOCRATES: Is it possible to manage a city well, or a household, or anything else, while not managing it moderately and justly? — Certainly not.

b   SOCRATES: Then if they manage justly and moderately, they must do so with justice and moderation? — Necessarily.

SOCRATES: So both the man and the woman, if they are to be good, need the same things, justice and moderation. — So it seems.

SOCRATES: What about a child and an old man? Can they possibly be good if they are intemperate and unjust? — Certainly not.

SOCRATES: But if they are moderate and just? — Yes.

c   SOCRATES: So all human beings are good in the same way, for they become good by acquiring the same qualities. — It seems so.

SOCRATES: And they would not be good in the same way if they did not have the same virtue. — They certainly would not be.

SOCRATES: Since then the virtue of all is the same, try to tell me and to remember what Gorgias, and you with him, said that that same thing is.

d   MENO: What else but to be able to rule over people, if you are seeking one description to fit them all.

SOCRATES: That is indeed what I am seeking, but, Meno, is virtue the same in the case of a child or a slave, namely, for them to be able to rule over a master, and do you think that he who rules is still a slave? — I do not think so at all, Socrates.

SOCRATES: It is not likely, my good man. Consider this further point: you say that virtue is to be able to rule. Shall we not add to this *justly and not unjustly?*

MENO: I think so, Socrates, for justice is virtue.

SOCRATES: Is it virtue, Meno, or a virtue? — What do you mean?   e

SOCRATES: As with anything else. For example, if you wish, take roundness, about which I would say that it is a shape, but not simply that it is shape. I would not so speak of it because there are other shapes.

MENO: You are quite right. So I too say that not only justice is a virtue but there are many other virtues.

SOCRATES: What are they? Tell me, as I could mention other shapes   74
to you if you bade me do so, so do you mention other virtues.

MENO: I think courage is a virtue, and moderation, wisdom, and munificence, and very many others.

SOCRATES: We are having the same trouble again, Meno, though in another way; we have found many virtues while looking for one, but we cannot find the one which covers all the others.

MENO: I cannot yet find, Socrates, what you are looking for, one   b
virtue for them all, as in the other cases.

SOCRATES: That is likely, but I am eager, if I can, that we should make progress, for you understand that the same applies to everything. If someone asked you what I mentioned just now: "What is shape, Meno?" and you told him that it was roundness, and if then he said to you what I did: "Is roundness shape or a shape?" you would surely tell him that it is a shape? — I certainly would.

SOCRATES: That would be because there are other shapes? — Yes.   c

SOCRATES: And if he asked you further what they were, you would tell him? — I would.

SOCRATES: So too, if he asked you what color is, and you said it is white, and your questioner interrupted you, "Is white color or a color?" you would say that it is a color, because there are also other colors? — I would.

SOCRATES: And if he bade you mention other colors, you would mention others that are no less colors than white is? — Yes.   d

SOCRATES: Then if he pursued the argument as I did and said: "We always arrive at the many; do not talk to me in that way, but since you call all these many by one name, and say that no one of them is not a shape even though they are opposites, tell me what this is which applies as much to the round as to the straight and which you call   e
shape, as you say the round is as much a shape as the straight." Do you not say that? — I do.

SOCRATES: When you speak like that, do you assert that the round is no more round than it is straight, and that the straight is no more straight than it is round?

MENO: Certainly not, Socrates.

SOCRATES: Yet you say that the round is no more a shape than the straight is, nor the one more than the other. — That is true.

SOCRATES: What then is this to which the name shape applies? Try to tell me. If then you answered the man who was questioning about shape or color: "I do not understand what you want, my man, nor what you mean," he would probably wonder and say: "You do not understand that I am seeking that which is the same in all these cases?" Would you still have nothing to say, Meno, if one asked you: "What is this which applies to the round and the straight and the other things which you call shapes and which is the same in them all?" Try to say, that you may practice for your answer about virtue.

MENO: No, Socrates, but you tell me.

SOCRATES: Do you want me to do you this favor?

MENO: I certainly do.

SOCRATES: And you will then be willing to tell me about virtue?

MENO: I will.

SOCRATES: We must certainly press on. The subject is worth it.

MENO: It surely is.

SOCRATES: Come then, let us try to tell you what shape is. See whether you will accept that it is this: Let us say that shape is that which alone of existing things always follows color. Is that satisfactory to you, or do you look for it in some other way? I should be satisfied if you defined virtue in this way.

MENO: But that is foolish, Socrates.

SOCRATES: How do you mean?

MENO: That shape, you say, always follows color. Well then, if someone were to say that he did not know what color is, but that he had the same difficulty as he had about shape, what do you think your answer would be?

SOCRATES: A true one, surely, and if my questioner was one of those clever and disputatious debaters, I would say to him: "I have given my answer; if it is wrong, it is your job to refute it." But if they are friends as you and I are, and want to discuss with each other, they must answer

in a manner more gentle and more proper to discussion. By this I mean
that the answers must not only be true, but in terms admittedly known
to the questioner. I too will try to speak in these terms. Do you call
something "the end"? I mean such a thing as a limit or boundary, for   e
all those are, I say, the same thing. Prodicus[1] might disagree with us,
but you surely call something "finished" or "completed"—that is what
I want to express, nothing elaborate.

MENO: I do, and I think I understand what you mean.

SOCRATES: Further, you call something a plane, and something else   76
a solid, as in geometry?

MENO: I do.

SOCRATES: From this you may understand what I mean by shape,
for I say this of every shape, that a shape is that which limits a solid;
in a word, a shape is the limit of a solid.

MENO: And what do you say color is, Socrates?

SOCRATES: You are outrageous, Meno. You bother an old man to
answer questions, but you yourself are not willing to recall and to tell   b
me what Gorgias says that virtue is.

MENO: After you have answered this, Socrates, I will tell you.

SOCRATES: Even someone who was blindfolded would know from
your conversation that you are handsome and still have lovers.

MENO: Why so?

SOCRATES: Because you are forever giving orders in a discussion, as
spoiled people do, who behave like tyrants as long as they are young.
And perhaps you have recognized that I am at a disadvantage with   c
handsome people, so I will do you the favor of an answer.

MENO: By all means do me that favor.

SOCRATES: Do you want me to answer after the manner of Gorgias,
which you would most easily follow?

MENO: Of course I want that.

SOCRATES: Do you both say there are effluvia of things, as Empedocles[2] does? — Certainly.

---

1. Prodicus was a well-known Sophist who was especially keen on the exact
meaning of words.

2. Empedocles (c. 493–433 B.C.) of Acragas in Sicily was a philosopher famous
for his theories about the world of nature and natural phenomena (including
sense-perception).

SOCRATES: And that there are channels through which the effluvia make their way? — Definitely.

d   SOCRATES: And some effluvia fit some of the channels, while others are too small or too big? — That is so.

SOCRATES: And there is something which you call sight? — There is.

SOCRATES: From this, "comprehend what I state," as Pindar said;[3] for color is an effluvium from shapes which fits the sight and is perceived.

MENO: That seems to me to be an excellent answer, Socrates.

SOCRATES: Perhaps it was given in the manner to which you are accustomed. At the same time I think that you can deduce from this answer what sound is, and smell, and many such things. — Quite so.

e

SOCRATES: It is a theatrical answer so it pleases you, Meno, more than that about shape. — It does.

SOCRATES: It is not better, son of Alexidemus, but I am convinced that the other is, and I think you would agree, if you did not have to go away before the mysteries as you told me yesterday, but could remain and be initiated.

MENO: I would stay, Socrates, if you could tell me many things like these.

77

SOCRATES: I shall certainly not be lacking in eagerness to tell you such things, both for your sake and my own, but I may not be able to tell you many. Come now, you too try to fulfill your promise to me and tell me the nature of virtue as a whole and stop making many out of one, as jokers say whenever someone breaks something; but allow virtue to remain whole and sound, and tell me what it is, for I have given you examples.

b

definition 3

MENO: I think, Socrates, that virtue is, as the poet says, "to find joy in beautiful things and have power." So I say that virtue is to desire beautiful things and have the power to acquire them.

SOCRATES: Do you mean that the man who desires beautiful things desires good things? — Most certainly.

SOCRATES: Do you assume that there are people who desire bad things, and others who desire good things? Do you not think, my good man, that all men desire good things?

c

---

3. Frg. 105 (Snell).

not knowingly does bad things → then every1 is equally virtuous.

MENO: I do not.

SOCRATES: But some desire bad things? — Yes.

SOCRATES: Do you mean that they believe the bad things to be good, or that they know they are bad and nevertheless desire them? — I think there are both kinds.

SOCRATES: Do you think, Meno, that anyone, knowing that bad things are bad, nevertheless desires them? — I certainly do.

SOCRATES: What do you mean by desiring? Is it to secure for oneself? — What else?

SOCRATES: Does he think that the bad things benefit him who possesses them, or does he know they harm him?   d

MENO: There are some who believe that the bad things benefit them, others who know that the bad things harm them.

SOCRATES: And do you think that those who believe that bad things benefit them know that they are bad?

MENO: No, that I cannot altogether believe.

SOCRATES: It is clear then that those who do not know things to be bad do not desire what is bad, but they desire those things that they   e believe to be good but that are in fact bad. It follows that those who have no knowledge of these things and believe them to be good clearly desire good things. Is that not so? — It is likely.

SOCRATES: Well then, those who you say desire bad things, believing that bad things harm their possessor, know that they will be harmed by them? — Necessarily.

SOCRATES: And do they not think that those who are harmed are   78 miserable to the extent that they are harmed? — That too is inevitable.

SOCRATES: And that those who are miserable are unhappy? — I think so.

SOCRATES: Does anyone wish to be miserable and unhappy? — I do not think so, Socrates.

SOCRATES: No one then wants what is bad, Meno, unless he wants to be such. For what else is being miserable but to desire bad things and secure them?

MENO: You are probably right, Socrates, and no one wants what   b is bad.

SOCRATES: Were you not saying just now that virtue is to desire good things and have the power to secure them? — Yes, I was.

SOCRATES: The desiring part of this statement is common to every-body, and one man is no better than another in this? — So it appears.

SOCRATES: Clearly then, if one man is better than another, he must be better at securing them. — Quite so.

c   SOCRATES: This then is virtue according to your argument, the power of securing good things.

MENO: I think, Socrates, that the case is altogether as you now understand it.

SOCRATES: Let us see then whether what you say is true, for you may well be right. You say that the capacity to acquire good things is virtue? — I do.

SOCRATES: And by good things you mean, for example, health and wealth?

MENO: Yes, and also to acquire gold and silver, also honors and offices in the city.

SOCRATES: By good things you do not mean other goods than these?

MENO: No, but I mean all things of this kind.

d   SOCRATES: Very well. According to Meno, the hereditary guest friend of the Great King, virtue is the acquisition of gold and silver. Do you add to this acquiring, Meno, the words justly and piously, or does it make no difference to you but even if one secures these things unjustly, you call it virtue nonetheless?

MENO: Certainly not, Socrates.

SOCRATES: You would then call it wickedness? — Indeed I would.

SOCRATES: It seems then that the acquisition must be accompanied

e   by justice or moderation or piety or some other part of virtue; if it is not, it will not be virtue, even though it provides good things.

MENO: How could there be virtue without these?

SOCRATES: Then failing to secure gold and silver, whenever it would not be just to do so, either for oneself or another, is not this failure to secure them also virtue?

MENO: So it seems.

SOCRATES: Then to provide these goods would not be virtue any

79   more than not to provide them, but apparently whatever is done with justice will be virtue, and what is done without anything of the kind is wickedness.

MENO: I think it must necessarily be as you say.

SOCRATES: We said a little while ago that each of these things was a part of virtue, namely, justice and moderation and all such things? — Yes.

SOCRATES: Then you are playing with me, Meno. — How so, Socrates?

SOCRATES: Because I begged you just now not to break up or fragment virtue, and I gave examples of how you should answer. You paid no attention, but you tell me that virtue is to be able to secure good things   b
with justice, and justice, you say, is a part of virtue.

MENO: I do.

SOCRATES: It follows then from what you agree to, that to act in whatever you do with a part of virtue is virtue, for you say that justice is a part of virtue, as are all such qualities. Why do I say this? Because when I begged you to tell me about virtue as a whole, you are far from telling me what it is. Rather, you say that every action is virtue if it is performed with a part of virtue, as if you had said what virtue is as a   c
whole, so I would already know that, even if you fragment it into parts. I think you must face the same question from the beginning, my dear Meno, namely, what is virtue, if every action performed with a part of virtue is virtue? For that is what one is saying when he says that every action performed with justice is virtue. Do you not think you should face the same question again, or do you think one knows what a part of virtue is if one does not know virtue itself? — I do not think so.

SOCRATES: If you remember, when I was answering you about shape,   d
we rejected the kind of answer that tried to answer in terms still being the subject of inquiry and not yet agreed upon. — And we were right to reject them.

SOCRATES: Then surely, my good sir, you must not think, while the nature of virtue as a whole is still under inquiry, that by answering in terms of the parts of virtue you can make its nature clear to anyone or make anything else clear by speaking in this way, but only that the same question must be put to you again—what do you take the nature   e
of virtue to be when you say what you say? Or do you think there is no point in what I am saying? — I think what you say is right.

SOCRATES: Answer me again then from the beginning: What do you and your friend say that virtue is?

MENO: Socrates, before I even met you I used to hear that you are   80
always in a state of perplexity and that you bring others to the same

state, and now I think you are bewitching and beguiling me, simply putting me under a spell, so that I am quite perplexed. Indeed, if a joke is in order, you seem, in appearance and in every other way, to be like the broad torpedo fish, for it too makes anyone who comes close and touches it feel numb, and you now seem to have had that kind of effect on me, for both my mind and my tongue are numb, and I have no answer to give you. Yet I have made many speeches about virtue before large audiences on a thousand occasions, very good speeches as I thought, but now I cannot even say what it is. I think you are wise not to sail away from Athens to go and stay elsewhere, for if you were to behave like this as a stranger in another city, you would be driven away for practicing sorcery.

SOCRATES: You are a rascal, Meno, and you nearly deceived me.

MENO: Why so particularly, Socrates?

SOCRATES: I know why you drew this image of me.

MENO: Why do you think I did?

SOCRATES: So that I should draw an image of you in return. I know that all handsome men rejoice in images of themselves; it is to their advantage, for I think that the images of beautiful people are also beautiful, but I will draw no image of you in turn. Now if the torpedo fish is itself numb and so makes others numb, then I resemble it, but not otherwise, for I myself do not have the answer when I perplex others, but I am more perplexed than anyone when I cause perplexity in others. So now I do not know what virtue is; perhaps you knew before you contacted me, but now you are certainly like one who does not know. Nevertheless, I want to examine and seek together with you what it may be.

MENO: How will you look for it, Socrates, when you do not know at all what it is? How will you aim to search for something you do not know at all? If you should meet with it, how will you know that this is the thing that you did not know?

SOCRATES: I know what you want to say, Meno. Do you realize what a debater's argument you are bringing up, that a man cannot search either for what he knows or for what he does not know? He cannot search for what he knows—since he knows it, there is no need to search—nor for what he does not know, for he does not know what to look for.

MENO: Does that argument not seem sound to you, Socrates?

SOCRATES: Not to me.

MENO: Can you tell me why?

SOCRATES: I can. I have heard wise men and women talk about divine matters . . .

MENO: What did they say?

SOCRATES: What was, I thought, both true and beautiful.

MENO: What was it, and who were they?

SOCRATES: The speakers were among the priests and priestesses whose care it is to be able to give an account of their practices. Pindar too   b
says it, and many others of the divine among our poets. What they say is this; see whether you think they speak the truth: They say that the human soul is immortal; at times it comes to an end, which they call dying; at times it is reborn, but it is never destroyed, and one must therefore live one's life as piously as possible:

> Persephone will return to the sun above in the ninth year
> the souls of those from whom
> she will exact punishment for old miseries,
> and from these come noble kings,   c
> mighty in strength and greatest in wisdom,
> and for the rest of time men will call them sacred heroes.[4]

As the soul is immortal, has been born often, and has seen all things here and in the underworld, there is nothing which it has not learned; so it is in no way surprising that it can recollect the things it knew before, both about virtue and other things. As the whole of nature is   d
akin, and the soul has learned everything, nothing prevents a man, after recalling one thing only—a process men call learning—discovering everything else for himself, if he is brave and does not tire of the search, for searching and learning are, as a whole, recollection. We must, therefore, not believe that debater's argument, for it would make us idle, and fainthearted men like to hear it, whereas my argument makes   e
them energetic and keen on the search. I trust that this is true, and I want to inquire along with you into the nature of virtue.

MENO: Yes, Socrates, but how do you mean that we do not learn, but that what we call learning is recollection? Can you teach me that this is so?

---

4. Frg. 133 (Snell).

82 SOCRATES: As I said just now, Meno, you are a rascal. You now ask me if I can teach you, when I say there is no teaching but recollection, in order to show me up at once as contradicting myself.

MENO: No, by Zeus, Socrates, that was not my intention when I spoke, but just a habit. If you can somehow show me that things are as you say, please do so.

b SOCRATES: It is not easy, but I am nevertheless willing to do my best for your sake. Call one of these many attendants of yours, whichever you like, that I may prove it to you in his case.

MENO: Certainly. You there come forward.

SOCRATES: Is he a Greek? Does he speak Greek?

MENO: Very much so. He was born in our household.

SOCRATES: Pay attention then whether you think he is recollecting or learning from me.

MENO: I will pay attention.

SOCRATES: Tell me now, boy, you know that a square figure is like this? — I do.

c SOCRATES: A square then is a figure in which all these four sides are equal? — Yes indeed.

SOCRATES: And it also has these lines through the middle equal?[5]—Yes.

---

5. Socrates draws a square ABCD. The "lines through the middle" are the lines joining the middle of these sides, which also go through the center of the square, namely EF and GH.

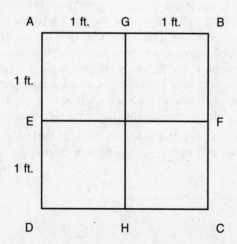

SOCRATES: And such a figure could be larger or smaller? — Certainly.

SOCRATES: If then this side were two feet, and this other side two feet, how many feet would the whole be? Consider it this way: If it were two feet this way, and only one foot that way, the figure would be once two feet? — Yes.

SOCRATES: But if it is two feet also that way, it would surely be twice two feet? — Yes.   d

SOCRATES: How many feet is twice two feet? Work it out and tell me. — Four, Socrates.

SOCRATES: Now we could have another figure twice the size of this one, with the four sides equal like this one. — Yes.

SOCRATES: How many feet will that be? — Eight.

SOCRATES: Come now, try to tell me how long each side of this will be. The side of this is two feet. What about each side of the one which is its double? — Obviously, Socrates, it will be twice the length.   e

SOCRATES: You see, Meno, that I am not teaching the boy anything, but all I do is question him. And now he thinks he knows the length of the line on which an eight-foot figure is based. Do you agree?

MENO: I do.

SOCRATES: And does he know?

MENO: Certainly not.

SOCRATES: He thinks it is a line twice the length?

MENO: Yes.

SOCRATES: Watch him now recollecting things in order, as one must recollect. Tell me, boy, do you say that a figure double the size is based on a line double the length? Now I mean such a figure as this, not   83
long on one side and short on the other, but equal in every direction like this one, and double the size, that is, eight feet. See whether you still believe that it will be based on a line double the length. — I do.

SOCRATES: Now the line becomes double its length if we add another of the same length here? — Yes indeed.

SOCRATES: And the eight-foot square will be based on it, if there are four lines of that length? — Yes.

SOCRATES: Well, let us draw from it four equal lines, and surely that   b
is what you say is the eight-foot square? — Certainly.

SOCRATES: And within this figure are four squares, each of which is equal to the four-foot square? — Yes.

SOCRATES: How big is it then? Is it not four times as big? — Of course.

SOCRATES: Is this square then, which is four times as big, its double? — No, by Zeus.

SOCRATES: How many times bigger is it? — Four times.

c   SOCRATES: Then, my boy, the figure based on a line twice the length is not double but four times as big? — You are right.

SOCRATES: And four times four is sixteen, is it not? — Yes.

SOCRATES: On how long a line should the eight-foot square be based? On *this* line we have a square that is four times bigger, do we not? — Yes.

SOCRATES: Now this four-foot square is based on this line here, half the length? — Yes.

SOCRATES: Very well. Is the eight-foot square not double this one and half that one?[6] — Yes.

d   SOCRATES: Will it not be based on a line longer than this one and shorter than that one? Is that not so? — I think so.

SOCRATES: Good, you answer what you think. And tell me, was this one not two-feet long, and that one four feet? — Yes.

SOCRATES: The line on which the eight-foot square is based must then be longer than this one of two feet, and shorter than that one of four feet? — It must be.

e   SOCRATES: Try to tell me then how long a line you say it is. — Three feet.

SOCRATES: Then if it is three feet, let us add the half of this one, and it will be three feet? For these are two feet, and the other is one. And here, similarly, these are two feet and that one is one foot, and so the figure you mention comes to be? — Yes.

SOCRATES: Now if it is three feet this way and three feet that way, will the whole figure be three times three feet? — So it seems.

SOCRATES: How much is three times three feet? — Nine feet.

SOCRATES: And the double square was to be how many feet? — Eight.

SOCRATES: So the eight-foot figure cannot be based on the three-foot line? — Clearly not.

---

6. I.e., the eight-foot square is double the four-foot square and half the sixteen-foot square—double the square based on a line two feet long and half the square based on a four-foot side.

SOCRATES: But on how long a line? Try to tell us exactly, and if you   84
do not want to work it out, show me from what line. — By Zeus,
Socrates, I do not know.

SOCRATES: You realize, Meno, what point he has reached in his
recollection. At first he did not know what the basic line of the eight-
foot square was; even now he does not yet know, but then he thought
he knew, and answered confidently as if he did know, and he did not
think himself at a loss, but now he does think himself at a loss, and as
he does not know, neither does he think he knows.   b

MENO: That is true.

SOCRATES: So he is now in a better position with regard to the matter
he does not know?

MENO: I agree with that too.

SOCRATES: Have we done him any harm by making him perplexed
and numb as the torpedo fish does?

MENO: I do not think so.

SOCRATES: Indeed, we have probably achieved something relevant
to finding out how matters stand, for now, as he does not know, he
would be glad to find out, whereas before he thought he could easily
make many fine speeches to large audiences about the square of double   c
size and said that it must have a base twice as long.

MENO: So it seems.

SOCRATES: Do you think that before he would have tried to find out
that which he thought he knew though he did not, before he fell into
perplexity and realized he did not know and longed to know?

MENO: I do not think so, Socrates.

SOCRATES: Has he then benefited from being numbed?

MENO: I think so.

SOCRATES: Look then how he will come out of his perplexity while
searching along with me. I shall do nothing more than ask questions
and not teach him. Watch whether you find me teaching and explaining   d
things to him instead of asking for his opinion.

SOCRATES: You tell me, is this not a four-foot figure? You understand? — I do.

SOCRATES: We add to it this figure which is equal to it? — Yes.

SOCRATES: And we add this third figure equal to each of them? — Yes.

SOCRATES: Could we then fill in the space in the corner? — Certainly.[7]

SOCRATES: So we have these four equal figures? — Yes.

e   SOCRATES: Well then, how many times is the whole figure larger than this one?[8] — Four times.

SOCRATES: But we should have had one that was twice as large, or do you not remember? — I certainly do.

85   SOCRATES: Does not this line from one corner to the other cut each of these figures in two?[9] — Yes.

---

7. Socrates now builds up his sixteen-foot square by joining two four-foot squares, then a third, like this:

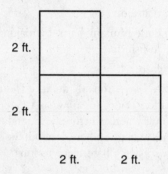

Filling "the space in the corner" will give another four-foot square, which completes the sixteen-foot square containing four four-foot squares.

8. "This one" is any one of the inside squares of four feet.

9. Socrates now draws the diagonals of the four inside squares, namely, FH, HE, EG, and GF, which together form the square GFHE.

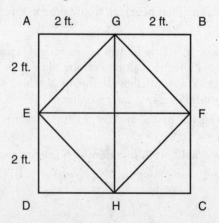

SOCRATES: So these are four equal lines which enclose this figure?[10] — They are.

SOCRATES: Consider now: How large is the figure? — I do not understand.

SOCRATES: Within these four figures, each line cuts off half of each, does it not? — Yes.

SOCRATES: How many of this size are there in this figure?[11] — Four.

SOCRATES: How many in this?[12] — Two.

SOCRATES: What is the relation of four to two? — Double.   b

SOCRATES: How many feet in this?[13] — Eight.

SOCRATES: Based on what line? — This one.

SOCRATES: That is, on the line that stretches from corner to corner of the four-foot figure? — Yes. — Clever men call this the diagonal, so that if diagonal is its name, you say that the double figure would be that based on the diagonal? — Most certainly, Socrates.

SOCRATES: What do you think, Meno? Has he, in his answers, expressed any opinion that was not his own?   c

MENO: No, they were all his own.

SOCRATES: And yet, as we said a short time ago, he did not know? — That is true.

SOCRATES: So these opinions were in him, were they not? — Yes.

SOCRATES: So the man who does not know has within himself true opinions about the things that he does not know? — So it appears.

SOCRATES: These opinions have now just been stirred up like a dream, but if he were repeatedly asked about these same things in various ways, you know that in the end his knowledge about these   d things would be as accurate as anyone's. — It is likely.

SOCRATES: And he will know it without having been taught but only questioned, and find the knowledge within himself? — Yes.

SOCRATES: And is not finding knowledge within oneself recollection? — Certainly.

---

10. I.e., GFHE.

11. Again, GFHE: Socrates is asking how many of the triangles "cut off from inside" there are inside GFHE.

12. I.e., any of the interior squares.

13. GFHE again.

SOCRATES: Must he not either have at some time acquired the knowledge he now possesses, or else have always possessed it? — Yes.

e   SOCRATES: If he always had it, he would always have known. If he acquired it, he cannot have done so in his present life. Or has someone taught him geometry? For he will perform in the same way about all geometry, and all other knowledge. Has someone taught him everything? You should know, especially as he has been born and brought up in your house.

MENO: But I know that no one has taught him.

SOCRATES: Yet he has these opinions, or doesn't he?

MENO: That seems indisputable, Socrates.

86   SOCRATES: If he has not acquired them in his present life, is it not clear that he had them and had learned them at some other time? — It seems so.

SOCRATES: Then that was the time when he was not a human being? — Yes.

SOCRATES: If then, during the time he exists and is not a human being he will have true opinions which, when stirred by questioning, become knowledge, will not his soul have learned during all time? For it is clear that during all time he exists, either as a man or not. — So it seems.

b   SOCRATES: Then if the truth about reality is always in our soul, the soul would be immortal so that you should always confidently try to seek out and recollect what you do not know at present—that is, what you do not recollect?

MENO: Somehow, Socrates, I think that what you say is right.

SOCRATES: I think so too, Meno. I do not insist that my argument is right in all other respects, but I would contend at all costs in both word and deed as far as I could that we will be better men, braver and less idle, if we believe that one must search for the things one does not

c   know, rather than if we believe that it is not possible to find out what we do not know and that we must not look for it.

MENO: In this too I think you are right, Socrates.

SOCRATES: Since we are of one mind that one should seek to find out what one does not know, shall we try to find out together what virtue is?

MENO: Certainly. But Socrates, I should be most pleased to investigate and hear your answer to my original question, whether we should

try to find out on the assumption that virtue is something teachable,   d
or is a natural gift, or in whatever way it comes to men.

SOCRATES: If I were directing you, Meno, and not only myself, we
would not investigate whether virtue is teachable or not before we
investigated what virtue itself is. But because you do not even attempt
to rule yourself, in order that you may be free, but you try to rule me
and do so, I will agree with you—for what can I do? So we must, it
appears, inquire into the qualities of something the nature of which   e
we do not yet know. However, please relax your rule a little bit for me
and agree to investigate whether it is teachable or not by means of a
hypothesis. I mean the way geometers often carry on their investigations.
For example, if they are asked whether a specific area can be inscribed   87
in the form of a triangle within a given circle, one of them might say:
"I do not yet know whether that area has that property, but I think I
have, as it were, a hypothesis that is of use for the problem, namely
this: If that area is such that when one has applied it as a rectangle to
the given straight line in the circle, it is deficient by a figure similar b
to the very figure which is applied, then I think one alternative results,
whereas another results if it is impossible for this to happen. So, by
using this hypothesis, I am willing to tell you what results with regard
to inscribing it in the circle—that is, whether it is impossible or not."[14]
So let us speak about virtue also, since we do not know either what it
is or what qualities it possesses, and let us investigate whether it is
teachable or not by means of a hypothesis, and say this: Among the
things existing in the soul, of what sort is virtue, that it should be
teachable or not? First, if it is another sort than knowledge, is it teachable
or not, or, as we were just saying, recollectable? Let it make no difference c
to us which term we use: Is it teachable? Or is it plain to anyone that
men cannot be taught anything but knowledge? — I think so.

SOCRATES: But, if virtue is a kind of knowledge, it is clear that it
could be taught. — Of course.

SOCRATES: We have dealt with that question quickly, that if it is of
one kind it can be taught; if it is of a different kind, it cannot. — We
have indeed.

SOCRATES: The next point to consider seems to be whether virtue
is knowledge or something else. — That does seem to be the next point d
to consider.

---

14. The translation here follows the interpretation of T. L. Heath, A *History
of Greek Mathematics* (Oxford: Clarendon Press, 1921), vol. I, pp. 298 ff.

SOCRATES: Well now, do we say that virtue is itself something good, and will this hypothesis stand firm for us, that it is something good? — Of course.

SOCRATES: If then there is anything else good that is different and separate from knowledge, virtue might well not be a kind of knowledge; but if there is nothing good that knowledge does not encompass, we would be right to suspect that it is a kind of knowledge. — That is so.

e   SOCRATES: Surely virtue makes us good? — Yes.

SOCRATES: And if we are good, we are beneficent, for all that is good is beneficial. Is that not so? — Yes.

SOCRATES: So virtue is something beneficial?

MENO: That necessarily follows from what has been agreed.

SOCRATES: Let us then examine what kinds of things benefit us, taking them up one by one: health, we say, and strength, and beauty, and also wealth. We say that these things, and others of the same kind, benefit us, do we not? — We do.

SOCRATES: Yet we say that these same things also sometimes harm
88   one. Do you agree or not? — I do.

SOCRATES: Look then, what directing factor determines in each case whether these things benefit or harm us? Is it not the right use of them that benefits us, and the wrong use that harms us? — Certainly.

SOCRATES: Let us now look at the qualities of the soul. There is something you call moderation, and justice, courage, mental quickness, memory, munificence, and all such things? — There is.

b   SOCRATES: Consider whichever of these you believe not to be knowledge but different from it; do they not at times harm us, at other times benefit us? Courage, for example, when it is not wisdom but like a kind of recklessness: when a man is reckless without understanding, he is harmed; when with understanding, he is benefited. — Yes.

SOCRATES: The same is true of moderation and mental quickness; when they are learned and disciplined with understanding they are beneficial, but without understanding they are harmful? — Very much so.

c   SOCRATES: Therefore, in a word, all that the soul undertakes and endures, if directed by wisdom, ends in happiness, but if directed by ignorance, it ends in the opposite? — That is likely.

SOCRATES: If then virtue is something in the soul and it must be beneficial, it must be knowledge, since all the qualities of the soul are

in themselves neither beneficial nor harmful, but accompanied by   d
wisdom or folly they become harmful or beneficial. This argument
shows that virtue, being beneficial, must be a kind of wisdom. — I agree.

SOCRATES: Furthermore, those other things we were mentioning just
now, wealth and the like, are at times good and at times harmful. Just
as for the rest of the soul the direction of wisdom makes things beneficial,
but harmful if directed by folly, so in these cases, if the soul uses and   e
directs them right it makes them beneficial, but bad use makes them
harmful? — Quite so.

SOCRATES: The wise soul directs them right, the foolish soul
wrongly? — That is so.

SOCRATES: So one may say this about everything; all other human
activities depend on the soul, and those of the soul itself depend on
wisdom if they are to be good. According to this argument the beneficial   89
would be wisdom, and we say that virtue is beneficial? — Certainly.

SOCRATES: Then we say that virtue is wisdom, either the whole or
a part of it?

MENO: What you say, Socrates, seems to me quite right.

SOCRATES: Then, if that is so, the good are not so by nature? — I
do not think they are.

SOCRATES: For if they were, this would follow: If the good were so   b
by nature, we would have people who knew which among the young
were by nature good; we would take those whom they had pointed out
and guard them in the Acropolis, sealing them up there much more
carefully than gold so that no one could corrupt them, and when they
reached maturity they would be useful to their cities. — Reasonable
enough, Socrates.

SOCRATES: Since the good are not good by nature, does learning   c
make them so?

MENO: Necessarily, as I now think, Socrates, and clearly, on our
hypothesis, if virtue is knowledge, it can be taught.

SOCRATES: Perhaps, by Zeus, but may it be that we were not right
to agree to this?

MENO: Yet it seemed to be right at the time.

SOCRATES: We should not only think it right at the time, but also
now and in the future if it is to be at all sound.

MENO: What is the difficulty? What do you have in mind that you   d
do not like about it and doubt that virtue is knowledge?

SOCRATES: I will tell you, Meno. I am not saying that it is wrong to say that virtue is teachable if it is knowledge, but look whether it is reasonable of me to doubt whether it is knowledge. Tell me this: If not only virtue but anything whatever can be taught, should there not be of necessity people who teach it and people who learn it? — I think so.

e   SOCRATES: Then again, if on the contrary there are no teachers or learners of something, we should be right to assume that the subject cannot be taught?

MENO: Quite so, but do you think that there are no teachers of virtue?

SOCRATES: I have often tried to find out whether there were any teachers of it, but in spite of all my efforts I cannot find any. And yet I have searched for them with the help of many people, especially those whom I believed to be most experienced in this matter. And now, Meno, Anytus[15] here has opportunely come to sit down by us. Let us

90 share our search with him. It would be reasonable for us to do so, for Anytus, in the first place, is the son of Anthemion, a man of wealth and wisdom, who did not become rich automatically or as the result of a gift like Ismenias the Theban, who recently acquired the possessions of Polycrates, but through his own wisdom and efforts. Further, he did not seem to be an arrogant or puffed up or offensive citizen in other

b   ways, but he was a well-mannered and well-behaved man. Also he gave our friend here a good upbringing and education, as the majority of Athenians believe, for they are electing him to the highest offices. It is right then to look for the teachers of virtue with the help of men such as he, whether there are any and if so who they are. Therefore, Anytus, please join me and your guest friend Meno here, in our inquiry as to who are the teachers of virtue. Look at it in this way: If we wanted

c   Meno to become a good physician, to what teachers would we send him? Would we not send him to the physicians?

ANYTUS: Certainly.

SOCRATES: And if we wanted him to be a good shoemaker, to shoe-makers? — Yes.

SOCRATES: And so with other pursuits? — Certainly.

SOCRATES: Tell me again on this same topic, like this: We say that we would be right to send him to the physicians if we want him to become a physician; whenever we say that, we mean that it would be

d

---

15. Anytus was one of Socrates' accusers at his trial. See *Apology* 23e.

reasonable to send him to those who practice the craft rather than to those who do not, and to those who exact fees for this very practice and have shown themselves to be teachers of anyone who wishes to come to them and learn. Is it not with this in mind that we would be right to send him? — Yes.

SOCRATES: And the same is true about flute-playing and the other crafts? It would be very foolish for those who want to make someone   e a flute-player to refuse to send him to those who profess to teach the craft and make money at it, but to send him to make trouble for others by seeking to learn from those who do not claim to be teachers or have a single pupil in that subject which we want the one we send to learn from them? Do you not think it very unreasonable to do so? — By Zeus, I do, and also very ignorant.

SOCRATES: Quite right. However, you can now deliberate with me about our guest friend Meno here. He has been telling me for some time, Anytus, that he longs to acquire that wisdom and virtue which   91 enables men to manage their households and their cities well, to take care of their parents, to know how to welcome and to send away both citizens and strangers as a good man should. Consider to whom we   b should be right to send him to learn this virtue. Or is it obvious in view of what was said just now that we should send him to those who profess to be teachers of virtue and have shown themselves to be available to any Greek who wishes to learn, and for this fix a fee and exact it?

ANYTUS: And who do you say these are, Socrates?

SOCRATES: You surely know yourself that they are those whom men call sophists.

ANYTUS: By Heracles, hush, Socrates. May no one of my household   c or friends, whether citizen or stranger, be mad enough to go to these people and be harmed by them, for they clearly cause the ruin and corruption of their followers.

SOCRATES: How do you mean, Anytus? Are these people, alone of those who claim the knowledge to benefit one, so different from the others that they not only do not benefit what one entrusts to them but on the contrary corrupt it, even though they obviously expect to make   d money from the process? I find I cannot believe you, for I know that one man, Protagoras, made more money from this knowledge of his than Phidias who made such notably fine works, and ten other sculptors. Surely what you say is extraordinary, if those who mend old sandals and restore clothes would be found out within the month if they returned   e the clothes and sandals in a worse state than they received them; if they did this they would soon die of starvation, but the whole of Greece has not noticed for forty years that Protagoras corrupts those who frequent him and sends them away in a worse moral condition than he received them. I believe that he was nearly seventy when he died and had practiced his craft for forty years. During all that time to this very day his reputation has stood high; and not only Protagoras but a great many others, some born before him and some still alive today. Are we to say that you maintain that they deceive and harm the young knowingly, or that they themselves are not aware of it? Are we to deem those whom some people consider the wisest of men to be so mad as that?

ANYTUS: They are far from being mad, Socrates. It is much rather those among the young who pay their fees who are mad, and even more the relatives who entrust their young to them and most of all the cities who allow them to come in and do not drive out any citizen or stranger who attempts to behave in this manner.

SOCRATES: Has some sophist wronged you, Anytus, or why are you so hard on them?

ANYTUS: No, by Zeus, I have never met one of them, nor would I allow any one of my people to do so.

SOCRATES: Are you then altogether without any experience of these men?

ANYTUS: And may I remain so.

SOCRATES: How then, my good sir, can you know whether there is any good in their instruction or not, if you are altogether without experience of it?

ANYTUS: Easily, for I know who they are, whether I have experience of them or not.

SOCRATES: Perhaps you are a wizard, Anytus, for I wonder, from what you yourself say, how else you know about these things. However, let us not try to find out who the men are whose company would make Meno wicked—let them be the sophists if you like—but tell us, and benefit your family friend here by telling him, to whom he should go in so large a city to acquire, to any worthwhile degree, the virtue I was just now describing.

ANYTUS: Why did you not tell him yourself?

SOCRATES: I did mention those whom I thought to be teachers of it, but you say I am wrong, and perhaps you are right. You tell him in your turn to whom among the Athenians he should go. Tell him the name of anyone you want.

ANYTUS: Why give him the name of one individual? Any Athenian gentleman he may meet, if he is willing to be persuaded, will make him a better man than the sophists would.

SOCRATES: And have these gentlemen become virtuous automatically, without learning from anyone, and are they able to teach others   93 what they themselves never learned?

ANYTUS: I believe that these men have learned from those who were gentlemen before them; or do you not think that there are many good men in this city?

SOCRATES: I believe, Anytus, that there are many men here who are good at public affairs, and that there have been as many in the past, but have they been good teachers of their own virtue? That is the point we are discussing, not whether there are good men here or not, or whether there have been in the past, but we have been investigating   b for some time whether virtue can be taught. And in the course of that investigation we are inquiring whether the good men of today and of the past knew how to pass on to another the virtue they themselves possessed, or whether a man cannot pass it on or receive it from another. This is what Meno and I have been investigating for some time. Look at it this way, from what you yourself have said. Would you not say that Themistocles[16] was a good man? — Yes. Even the best of men.   c

SOCRATES: And therefore a good teacher of his own virtue if anyone was?

ANYTUS: I think so, if he wanted to be.

SOCRATES: But do you think he did not want some other people to be worthy men, and especially his own son? Or do you think he begrudged him this, and deliberately did not pass on to him his own virtue?   d Have you not heard that Themistocles taught his son Cleophantus to be a good horseman? He could remain standing upright on horseback and shoot javelins from that position and do many other remarkable things which his father had him taught and made skillful at, all of which required good teachers. Have you not heard this from your elders? — I have.

---

16. Famous Athenian statesman and general of the early fifth century B.C., a leader in the victorious war against the Persians.

SOCRATES: So one could not blame the poor natural talents of the
e   son for his failure in virtue? — Perhaps not.

SOCRATES: But have you ever heard anyone, young or old, say that
Cleophantus, the son of Themistocles, was a good and wise man at the
same pursuits as his father? — Never.

SOCRATES: Are we to believe that he wanted to educate his son in
those other things but not to do better than his neighbors in that skill
which he himself possessed, if indeed virtue can be taught? — Perhaps
not, by Zeus.

SOCRATES: And yet he was, as you yourself agree, among the best
94   teachers of virtue in the past. Let us consider another man, Aristides,
the son of Lysimachus. Do you not agree that he was good? — I very
definitely do.

SOCRATES: He too gave his own son Lysimachus the best Athenian
education in matters which are the business of teachers, and do you
think he made him a better man than anyone else? For you have been
b   in his company and seen the kind of man he is. Or take Pericles, a
man of such magnificent wisdom. You know that he brought up two
sons, Paralus and Xanthippus? — I know.

SOCRATES: You also know that he taught them to be as good horsemen
as any Athenian, that he educated them in the arts, in gymnastics, and
in all else that was a matter of skill not to be inferior to anyone, but
did he not want to make them good men? I think he did, but this could
not be taught. And lest you think that only a few most inferior Athenians
are incapable in this respect, reflect that Thucydides[17] too brought up
c   two sons, Melesias and Stephanus, that he educated them well in all
other things. They were the best wrestlers in Athens—he entrusted the
one to Xanthias and the other to Eudorus, who were thought to be the
best wrestlers of the day, or do you not remember?

ANYTUS: I remember I have heard that said.

d   SOCRATES: It is surely clear that he would not have taught his boys
what it costs money to teach, but have failed to teach them what costs
nothing—making them good men—if that could be taught? Or was
Thucydides perhaps an inferior person who had not many friends among
the Athenians and the allies? He belonged to a great house; he had

---

17. Not the historian but Thucydides the son of Melesias, an Athenian statesman who was an opponent of Pericles and who was ostracized in 440 B.C.

great influence in the city and among the other Greeks, so that if virtue could be taught he would have found the man who could make his sons good men, be it a citizen or a stranger, if he himself did not have the time because of his public concerns. But, friend Anytus, virtue can certainly not be taught.

ANYTUS: I think, Socrates, that you easily speak ill of people. I would advise you, if you will listen to me, to be careful. Perhaps also in another city, and certainly here, it is easier to injure people than to benefit them. I think you know that yourself.

SOCRATES: I think, Meno, that Anytus is angry, and I am not at all surprised. He thinks, to begin with, that I am slandering those men, and then he believes himself to be one of them. If he ever realizes what slander is, he will cease from anger, but he does not know it now. You tell me, are there not worthy men among your people? — Certainly.

SOCRATES: Well now, are they willing to offer themselves to the young as teachers? Do they agree they are teachers, and that virtue can be taught?

MENO: No, by Zeus, Socrates, but sometimes you would hear them say that it can be taught, at other times, that it cannot.

SOCRATES: Should we say that they are teachers of this subject, when they do not even agree on this point? — I do not think so, Socrates.

SOCRATES: Further, do you think that these sophists, who alone profess to be so, are teachers of virtue?

MENO: I admire this most in Gorgias, Socrates, that you would never hear him promising this. Indeed, he ridicules the others when he hears them making this claim. He thinks one should make people clever speakers.

SOCRATES: You do not think then that the sophists are teachers?

MENO: I cannot tell, Socrates; like most people, at times I think they are; at other times I think that they are not.

SOCRATES: Do you know that not only you and the other public men at times think that it can be taught, at other times that it cannot, but that the poet Theognis[18] says the same thing? — Where?

SOCRATES: In his elegiacs: "Eat and drink with these men, and keep their company. Please those whose power is great, for you will learn

---

18. Theognis was a poet of the mid–sixth century B.C. The quotations below are of lines 33–36 and 434–38 (Diehl) of his elegies.

e   goodness from the good. If you mingle with bad men you will lose even what wit you possess." You see that here he speaks as if virtue can be taught? — So it appears.

SOCRATES: Elsewhere, he changes somewhat: "If this could be done," he says, "and intelligence could be instilled," somehow those who could do this "would collect large and numerous fees," and further: "Never would a bad son be born of a good father, for he would be persuaded

96   by wise words, but you will never make a bad man good by teaching." You realize that the poet is contradicting himself on the same subject? — He seems to be.

SOCRATES: Can you mention any other subject of which those who claim to be teachers not only are not recognized to be teachers of others but are not recognized to have knowledge of it themselves, and are

b   thought to be poor in the very matter which they profess to teach? Or any other subject of which those who are recognized as worthy teachers at one time say it can be taught and at other times that it cannot? Would you say that people who are so confused about a subject can be effective teachers of it? — No, by Zeus, I would not.

SOCRATES: If then neither the sophists nor the worthy people themselves are teachers of this subject, clearly there would be no others? — I do not think there are.

c   SOCRATES: If there are no teachers, neither are there pupils? — As you say.

SOCRATES: And we agreed that a subject that has neither teachers nor pupils is not teachable? — We have so agreed.

SOCRATES: Now there seem to be no teachers of virtue anywhere? — That is so.

SOCRATES: If there are no teachers, there are no learners? — That seems so.

SOCRATES: Then virtue cannot be taught?

d   MENO: Apparently not, if we have investigated this correctly. I certainly wonder, Socrates, whether there are no good men either, or in what way good men come to be.

SOCRATES: We are probably poor specimens, you and I, Meno. Gorgias has not adequately educated you, nor Prodicus me. We must then at all costs turn our attention to ourselves and find someone who

e   will in some way make us better. I say this in view of our recent investigation, for it is ridiculous that we failed to see that it is not only under the direction of knowledge that men succeed in their affairs, and that is perhaps why the knowledge of how good men come to be escapes us.

MENO: How do you mean, Socrates?

SOCRATES: I mean this: We were right to agree that good men must be beneficent, and that this could not be otherwise. Is that not so? — Yes.

SOCRATES: And that they will be beneficent if they give us correct direction in our affairs. To this too we were right to agree? — Yes.   97

SOCRATES: But that one cannot give correct direction if one does not have knowledge; to this our agreement is likely to be incorrect. — How do you mean?

SOCRATES: I will tell you. A man who knew the way to Larissa, or anywhere else you like, and went there and directed others would surely lead them well and correctly? — Certainly.

SOCRATES: What if someone had had a correct opinion as to which   b was the way but had not gone there nor indeed had knowledge of it, would he not also lead correctly? — Certainly.

SOCRATES: And as long as he has the right opinion about that of which the other has knowledge, he will not be a worse guide than the one who knows, as he has a true opinion, though not knowledge. — In no way worse.

SOCRATES: So true opinion is in no way a worse guide for correct action than knowledge. It is this that we omitted in our investigation of the nature of virtue, when we said that only knowledge can guide   c correct action, for true opinion can do so also. — So it seems.

SOCRATES: So correct opinion is no less useful than knowledge?

MENO: Yes, to this extent, Socrates. But the man who has knowledge will always succeed, whereas he who has true opinion will only succeed at times.

SOCRATES: How do you mean? Will he who has the right opinion not always succeed, as long as his opinion is right?

MENO: That appears to be so of necessity, and it makes me wonder, Socrates, this being the case, why knowledge is prized far more highly   d than right opinion, and why they are different.

SOCRATES: Do you know why you wonder, or shall I tell you? — By all means tell me.

SOCRATES: It is because you have paid no attention to the statues of Daedalus, but perhaps there are none in Thessaly.

MENO: What do you have in mind when you say this?

SOCRATES: That they too run away and escape if one does not tie
e   them down but remain in place if tied down. — So what?

SOCRATES: To acquire an untied work of Daedalus is not worth
much, like acquiring a runaway slave, for it does not remain, but it is
worth much if tied down, for his works are very beautiful. What am I
thinking of when I say this? True opinions. For true opinions, as long
as they remain, are a fine thing and all they do is good, but they are
98   not willing to remain long, and they escape from a man's mind, so that
they are not worth much until one ties them down by [giving] an
account of the reason why. And that, Meno, my friend, is recollection,
as we previously agreed. After they are tied down, in the first place
they become knowledge, and then they remain in place. That is why
knowledge is prized higher than correct opinion, and knowledge differs
from correct opinion in being tied down.

MENO: Yes, by Zeus, Socrates, it seems to be something like that.

b   SOCRATES: Indeed, I too speak as one who does not have knowledge
but is guessing. However, I certainly do not think I am guessing that
right opinion is a different thing from knowledge. If I claim to know
anything else—and I would make that claim about few things—I would
put this down as one of the things I know. — Rightly so, Socrates.

SOCRATES: Well then, is it not correct that when true opinion guides
the course of every action, it does no worse than knowledge? — I think
you are right in this too.

c   SOCRATES: Correct opinion is then neither inferior to knowledge
nor less useful in directing actions, nor is the man who has it less so
than he who has knowledge. — That is so.

SOCRATES: And we agreed that the good man is beneficent. — Yes.

SOCRATES: Since then it is not only through knowledge but also
through right opinion that men are good, and beneficial to their cities
d   when they are, and neither knowledge nor true opinion come to men
by nature but are acquired—or do you think either of these comes by
nature? — I do not think so.

SOCRATES: Then if they do not come by nature, men are not so by
nature either. — Surely not.

SOCRATES: As goodness does not come by nature, we inquired next
whether it could be taught. — Yes.

SOCRATES: We thought it could be taught, if it was knowledge? — Yes.

SOCRATES: And that it was knowledge if it could be taught? — Quite so.

SOCRATES: And that if there were teachers of it, it could be taught,   e
but if there were not, it was not teachable? — That is so.

SOCRATES: And then we agreed that there were no teachers of it? — We did.

SOCRATES: So we agreed that it was neither teachable nor knowledge? — Quite so.

SOCRATES: But we certainly agree that virtue is a good thing? — Yes.

SOCRATES: And that which guides correctly is both useful and good? — Certainly.

SOCRATES: And that only these two things, true belief and knowledge,   99
guide correctly, and that if a man possesses these he gives correct guidance. The things that turn out right by some chance are not due to human guidance, but where there is correct human guidance it is due to two things, true belief or knowledge. — I think that is so.

SOCRATES: Now because it cannot be taught, virtue no longer seems to be knowledge? — It seems not.

SOCRATES: So one of the two good and useful things has been   b
excluded, and knowledge is not the guide in public affairs. — I do not think so.

SOCRATES: So it is not by some kind of wisdom, or by being wise, that such men lead their cities, those such as Themistocles and those mentioned by Anytus just now? That is the reason why they cannot make others be like themselves, because it is not knowledge which makes them what they are.

MENO: It is likely to be as you say, Socrates.

SOCRATES: Therefore, if it is not through knowledge, the only alternative is that it is through right opinion that statesmen follow the right   c
course for their cities. As regards knowledge, they are no different from soothsayers and prophets. They too say many true things when inspired, but they have no knowledge of what they are saying. — That is probably so.

SOCRATES: And so, Meno, is it right to call divine these men who, without any understanding, are right in much that is of importance in what they say and do? — Certainly.

SOCRATES: We should be right to call divine also those soothsayers and prophets whom we just mentioned, and all the poets, and we   d should call no less divine and inspired those public men who are no less under the gods' influence and possession, as their speeches lead to success in many important matters, though they have no knowledge of what they are saying. — Quite so.

SOCRATES: Women too, Meno, call good men divine, and the Spartans, when they eulogize someone, say "This man is divine."

e   MENO: And they appear to be right, Socrates, though perhaps Anytus here will be annoyed with you for saying so.

SOCRATES: I do not mind that; we shall talk to him again, but if we were right in the way in which we spoke and investigated in this whole discussion, virtue would be neither an inborn quality nor taught, but comes to those who possess it as a gift from the gods which is not 100   accompanied by understanding, unless there is someone among our statesmen who can make another into a statesman. If there were one, he could be said to be among the living as Homer said Tiresias was among the dead, namely, that "he alone retained his wits while the others flitted about like shadows."[19] In the same manner such a man would, as far as virtue is concerned, here also be the only true reality compared, as it were, with shadows.

b   MENO: I think that is an excellent way to put it, Socrates.

SOCRATES: It follows from this reasoning, Meno, that virtue appears to be present in those of us who may possess it as a gift from the gods. We shall have clear knowledge of this when, before we investigate how it comes to be present in men, we first try to find out what virtue in itself is. But now the time has come for me to go. You convince your guest friend Anytus here of these very things of which you have yourself been convinced, in order that he may be more amenable. If you succeed, you will also confer a benefit upon the Athenians.

---

19. *Odyssey* x.494–95.

PHAEDO

Phaedo, *known to the ancients also by the descriptive title* On the Soul, *is a drama about Socrates' last hours and his death in the jail at Athens. On the way back home to Elis, one of his intimates, Phaedo, who was with him then, stops off at Phlius, in the Peloponnese. There he reports it all to a group of Pythagoreans settled there since their expulsion from southern Italy. The Pythagorean connection is carried further in the dialogue itself, since Socrates' two fellow discussants, Simmias and Cebes—from Thebes, the other city where expelled members of the brotherhood settled—are associates of Philolaus, the leading Pythagorean there. Pythagoreans were noted for their belief in the immortality of the soul and its reincarnation in human or animal form and for the consequent concern to keep one's soul pure by avoiding contamination with the body, so as to win the best possible next life. Socrates weaves all these themes into his own discussion of the immortality of the soul.*

It is noteworthy that these Pythagorean elements are lacking from the Apology, *where Socrates expresses himself noncommittally and unconcernedly about the possibility of immortality—and from* Crito, *as well as the varied discussions of the soul's virtues in such dialogues as* Euthyphro, Laches, *and* Protagoras. *Those dialogues are of course not records of discussions the historical Socrates actually held, but Plato seems to take particular pains to indicate that* Phaedo *does not give us Socrates' actual last conversation or even one that fits at all closely his actual views. He takes care to tell us that he was not present on the last day: Phaedo says he was ill. Socrates makes much of the human intellect's affinity to eternal Forms of Beauty, Justice, and other normative notions, and of mathematical properties and objects, such as Oddness and Evenness and the integers Two, Three, and the rest, as well as physical forces such as Hot and Cold, all existing in a nonphysical realm accessible only to abstract thought. None of this comports well with Socrates' description of his philosophical interests in the* Apology *or with the way he conducts his inquiries in Plato's "Socratic" dialogues. It is generally agreed that both the Pythagorean motifs of immortality and purification and the*

*theory of eternal Forms that is linked with them in this dialogue are
Plato's own contribution. Indeed, Phaedo's affinities in philosophical
theory go not towards the Socratic dialogues, but to* Symposium *and*
Republic. *There is an unmistakable reference to* Meno's *theory of
theoretical knowledge (of geometry, and also of the nature of human
virtue) as coming by recollection of objects known before birth. But
now the claim is made that this recollection is of Forms.*

*Phaedo concludes with a myth describing the fate of the soul after
death. Concluding myths in other dialogues, with which this one
should be compared, are those in* Gorgias *and* Republic. *It should
also be compared with the myth in Socrates' second speech in*
Phaedrus.

Despite the Platonic innovations in philosophical theory, Phaedo
*presents a famously moving picture of Socrates' deep commitment to
philosophy and the philosophical life even, or especially, in the face of
an unjustly imposed death.*

J.M.C.

57   ECHECRATES: Were you with Socrates yourself, Phaedo, on the day
when he drank the poison in prison, or did someone else tell you
about it?

PHAEDO: I was there myself, Echecrates.

ECHECRATES: What are the things he said before he died? And how
did he die? I should be glad to hear this. Hardly anyone from Phlius
b   visits Athens nowadays, nor has any stranger come from Athens for
some time who could give us a clear account of what happened, except
that he drank the poison and died, but nothing more.

58   PHAEDO: Did you not even hear how the trial went?

ECHECRATES: Yes, someone did tell us about that, and we wondered
that he seems to have died a long time after the trial took place. Why
was that, Phaedo?

PHAEDO: That was by chance, Echecrates. The day before the trial,
as it happened, the prow of the ship that the Athenians send to Delos
had been crowned with garlands.

ECHECRATES: What ship is that?

PHAEDO: It is the ship in which, the Athenians say, Theseus once sailed to Crete, taking with him the two lots of seven victims.[1] He saved them and was himself saved. The Athenians vowed then to Apollo, so the story goes, that if they were saved they would send a mission to Delos every year. And from that time to this they send such an annual mission to the god. They have a law to keep the city pure while it lasts, and no execution may take place once the mission has begun until the ship has made its journey to Delos and returned to Athens, and this can sometimes take a long time if the winds delay it. The mission begins when the priest of Apollo crowns the prow of the ship, and this happened, as I say, the day before Socrates' trial. That is why Socrates was in prison a long time between his trial and his execution.

ECHECRATES: What about his actual death, Phaedo? What did he say? What did he do? Who of his friends were with him? Or did the authorities not allow them to be present and he died with no friends present?

PHAEDO: By no means. Some were present, in fact, a good many.

ECHECRATES: Please be good enough to tell us all that occurred as fully as possible, unless you have some pressing business.

PHAEDO: I have the time and I will try to tell you the whole story, for nothing gives me more pleasure than to call Socrates to mind, whether talking about him myself, or listening to someone else do so.

ECHECRATES: Your hearers will surely be like you in this, Phaedo. So do try to tell us every detail as exactly as you can.

PHAEDO: I certainly found being there an astonishing experience. Although I was witnessing the death of one who was my friend, I had no feeling of pity, for the man appeared happy in both manner and words as he died nobly and without fear, Echecrates, so that it struck me that even in going down to the underworld he was going with the gods' blessing and that he would fare well when he got there, if anyone ever does. That is why I had no feeling of pity, such as would seem natural in my sorrow, nor indeed of pleasure, as we engaged in philosophical discussion as we were accustomed to do—for our arguments were of that sort—but I had a strange feeling, an unaccustomed mixture of pleasure and pain at the same time as I reflected that he was just

1. Legend says that Minos, king of Crete, compelled the Athenians to send seven youths and seven maidens every year to be sacrificed to the Minotaur until Theseus saved them and killed the monster.

about to die. All of us present were affected in much the same way,
sometimes laughing, then weeping; especially one of us, Apollodorus—
you know the man and his ways.

b   ECHECRATES: Of course I do.

PHAEDO: He was quite overcome; but I was myself disturbed, and
so were the others.

ECHECRATES: Who, Phaedo, were those present?

PHAEDO: Among the local people there was Apollodorus, whom I
mentioned, Critobulus and his father,[2] also Hermogenes, Epigenes,
Aeschines, and Antisthenes. Ctesippus of Paeania was there, Menexenus
and some others. Plato, I believe, was ill.

ECHECRATES: Were there some foreigners present?

c   PHAEDO: Yes, Simmias from Thebes with Cebes and Phaedondes,
and from Megara, Euclides and Terpsion.

ECHECRATES: What about Aristippus and Cleombrotus? Were they
there?

PHAEDO: No. They were said to be in Aegina.

ECHECRATES: Was there anyone else?

PHAEDO: I think these were about all.

ECHECRATES: Well then, what do you say the conversation was about?

PHAEDO: I will try to tell you everything from the beginning. On
d   the previous days also both the others and I used to visit Socrates. We
foregathered at daybreak at the court where the trial took place, for it
was close to the prison, and each day we used to wait around talking
until the prison should open, for it did not open early. When it opened
we used to go in to Socrates and spend most of the day with him. On
e   this day we gathered rather early, because when we left the prison on
the previous evening we were informed that the ship from Delos had

---

2. The father of Critobulus is Crito, after whom the dialogue *Crito* is named.
Several of the other friends of Socrates mentioned here also appear in other
dialogues. Hermogenes is one of the speakers in *Cratylus*. Epigenes is mentioned
in *Apology* 33e, as is Aeschines, who was a writer of Socratic dialogues. Menexenus has a part in *Lysis* and has a dialogue named after him; Ctesippus appears
in both *Lysis* and *Euthydemus*. Euclides and Terpsion are speakers in the
introductory conversation of *Theaetetus*, and Euclides too wrote Socratic dialogues. Simmias and Cebes are mentioned in *Crito* 45b as having come to
Athens with enough money to secure Socrates' escape.

arrived, and so we told each other to come to the usual place as early
as possible. When we arrived the gatekeeper who used to answer our
knock came out and told us to wait and not go in until he told us to.
"The Eleven,"[3] he said, "are freeing Socrates from his bonds and telling
him how his death will take place today." After a short time he came
and told us to go in. We found Socrates recently released from his   60
chains, and Xanthippe—you know her—sitting by him, holding their
baby. When she saw us, she cried out and said the sort of thing that
women usually say: "Socrates, this is the last time your friends will talk
to you and you to them." Socrates looked at Crito. "Crito," he said,
"let someone take her home." And some of Crito's people led her away
lamenting and beating her breast.   b

Socrates sat up on the bed, bent his leg, and rubbed it with his hand,
and as he rubbed he said: "What a strange thing that which men call
pleasure seems to be, and how astonishing the relation it has with what
is thought to be its opposite, namely pain! A man cannot have both at
the same time. Yet if he pursues and catches the one, he is almost
always bound to catch the other also, like two creatures with one head.
I think that if Aesop had noted this he would have composed a fable   c
that a god wished to reconcile their opposition but could not do so, so
he joined their two heads together, and therefore when a man has the
one, the other follows later. This seems to be happening to me. My
bonds caused pain in my leg, and now pleasure seems to be following."

Cebes intervened and said: "By Zeus, yes, Socrates, you did well to
remind me. Evenus[4] asked me the day before yesterday, as others had
done before, what induced you to write poetry after you came to prison,   d
you who had never composed any poetry before, putting the fables of
Aesop into verse and composing the hymn to Apollo. If it is of any
concern to you that I should have an answer to give to Evenus when
he repeats his question, as I know he will, tell me what to say to him."

Tell him the truth, Cebes, he said, that I did not do this with the
idea of rivaling him or his poems, for I knew that would not be easy,
but I tried to find out the meaning of certain dreams and to satisfy my   e
conscience in case it was this kind of art they were frequently bidding
me to practice. The dreams were something like this: the same dream

---

3. The Eleven were the police commissioners of Athens.
4. Socrates refers to Evenus as a Sophist and teacher of the young in *Apology* 20a–c.

often came to me in the past, now in one shape now in another, but
saying the same thing: "Socrates," it said, "practice and cultivate the
arts." In the past I imagined that it was instructing and advising me to
do what I was doing, such as those who encourage runners in a race,
61   that the dream was thus bidding me do the very thing I was doing,
namely, to practice the art of philosophy, this being the highest kind
of art, and I was doing that.

But now, after my trial took place, and the festival of the god was
preventing my execution, I thought that, in case my dream was bidding
me to practice this popular art, I should not disobey it but compose
b   poetry. I thought it safer not to leave here until I had satisfied my
conscience by writing poems in obedience to the dream. So I first wrote
in honor of the god of the present festival. After that I realized that a
poet, if he is to be a poet, must compose fables, not arguments. Being
no teller of fables myself, I took the stories I knew and had at hand,
the fables of Aesop, and I versified the first ones I came across. Tell
this to Evenus, Cebes, wish him well and bid him farewell, and tell
him, if he is wise, to follow me as soon as possible. I am leaving today,
c   it seems, as the Athenians so order it.

Said Simmias: "What kind of advice is this you are giving to Evenus,
Socrates? I have met him many times, and from my observation he is
not at all likely to follow it willingly."

How so, said he, is Evenus not a philosopher?

I think so, Simmias said.

Then Evenus will be willing, like every man who partakes worthily
of philosophy. Yet perhaps he will not take his own life, for that, they
d   say, is not right. As he said this, Socrates put his feet on the ground
and remained in this position during the rest of the conversation.

Then Cebes asked: "How do you mean Socrates, that it is not right
to do oneself violence, and yet that the philosopher will be willing to
follow one who is dying?"

Come now, Cebes, have you and Simmias, who keep company with
Philolaus,[5] not heard about such things?

Nothing definite, Socrates.

Indeed, I too speak about this from hearsay, but I do not mind telling
you what I have heard, for it is perhaps most appropriate for one who
e   is about to depart yonder to tell and examine tales about what we

---

5. See the introduction to this dialogue.

believe that journey to be like. What else could one do in the time we have until sunset?

But whatever is the reason, Socrates, for people to say that it is not right to kill oneself? As to your question just now, I have heard Philolaus say this when staying in Thebes and I have also heard it from others, but I have never heard anyone give a clear account of the matter.

Well, he said, we must do our best, and you may yet hear one. And 62 it may well astonish you if this subject, alone of all things, is simple, and it is never, as with everything else, better at certain times and for certain people to die than to live. And if this is so, you may well find it astonishing that those for whom it is better to die are wrong to help themselves, and that they must wait for someone else to benefit them.

And Cebes, lapsing into his own dialect, laughed quietly and said: "Zeus knows it is."

Indeed, said Socrates, it does seem unreasonable when put like that, b but perhaps there is reason to it. There is the explanation that is put in the language of the mysteries, that we men are in a kind of prison, and that one must not free oneself or run away. That seems to me an impressive doctrine and one not easy to understand fully. However, Cebes, this seems to me well expressed, that the gods are our guardians and that men are one of their possessions. Or do you not think so?

I do, said Cebes.

And would you not be angry if one of your possessions killed itself when you had not given any sign that you wished it to die, and if you c had any punishment you could inflict, you would inflict it?

Certainly, he said.

Perhaps then, put in this way, it is not unreasonable that one should not kill oneself before a god had indicated some necessity to do so, like the necessity now put upon us.

That seems likely, said Cebes. As for what you were saying, that d philosophers should be willing and ready to die, that seems strange, Socrates, if what we said just now is reasonable, namely, that a god is our protector and that we are his possessions. It is not logical that the wisest of men should not resent leaving this service in which they are governed by the best of masters, the gods, for a wise man cannot believe that he will look after himself better when he is free. A foolish man might easily think so, that he must escape from his master; he would e not reflect that one must not escape from a good master but stay with him as long as possible, because it would be foolish to escape. But the sensible man would want always to remain with one better than himself.

So, Socrates, the opposite of what was said before is likely to be true; the wise would resent dying, whereas the foolish would rejoice at it.

I thought that when Socrates heard this he was pleased by Cebes' argumentation. Glancing at us, he said: "Cebes is always on the track of some arguments; he is certainly not willing to be at once convinced by what one says."

Said Simmias: "But actually, Socrates, I think myself that Cebes has a point now. Why should truly wise men want to avoid the service of masters better than themselves, and leave them easily? And I think Cebes is aiming his argument at you, because you are bearing leaving us so lightly, and leaving those good masters, as you say yourself, the gods."

You are both justified in what you say, and I think you mean that I must make a defense against this, as if I were in court.

You certainly must, said Simmias.

Come then, he said, let me try to make my defense to you more convincing than it was to the jury. For, Simmias and Cebes, I should be wrong not to resent dying if I did not believe that I should go first to other wise and good gods, and then to men who have died and are better than men are here. Be assured that, as it is, I expect to join the company of good men. This last I would not altogether insist on, but if I insist on anything at all in these matters, it is that I shall come to gods who are very good masters. That is why I am not so resentful, because I have good hope that some future awaits men after death, as we have been told for years, a much better future for the good than for the wicked.

Well now, Socrates, said Simmias, do you intend to keep this belief to yourself as you leave us, or would you share it with us? I certainly think it would be a blessing for us too, and at the same time it would be your defense if you convince us of what you say.

I will try, he said, but first let us see what it is that Crito here has, I think, been wanting to say for quite a while.

What else, Socrates, said Crito, but what the man who is to give you the poison has been telling me for some time, that I should warn you to talk as little as possible. People get heated when they talk, he says, and one should not be heated when taking the poison, as those who do must sometimes drink it two or three times.

Socrates replied: "Take no notice of him; only let him be prepared to administer it twice or, if necessary, three times."

I was rather sure you would say that, Crito said, but he has been bothering me for some time.

Let him be, he said. I want to make my argument before you, my judges, as to why I think that a man who has truly spent his life in philosophy is probably right to be of good cheer in the face of death and to be very hopeful that after death he will attain the greatest blessings yonder. I will try to tell you, Simmias and Cebes, how this may be so. I am afraid that other people do not realize that the one aim of those who practice philosophy in the proper manner is to practice for dying and death. Now if this is true, it would be strange indeed if they were eager for this all their lives and then resent it when what they have wanted and practiced for a long time comes upon them.

64

Simmias laughed and said: "By Zeus, Socrates, you made me laugh, though I was in no laughing mood just now. I think that the majority, on hearing this, will think that it describes the philosophers very well, and our people in Thebes would thoroughly agree that philosophers are nearly dead and that the majority of men is well aware that they deserve to be.

b

And they would be telling the truth, Simmias, except for their being aware. They are not aware of the way true philosophers are nearly dead, nor of the way they deserve to be, nor of the sort of death they deserve. But never mind them, he said, let us talk among ourselves. Do we believe that there is such a thing as death?

c

Certainly, said Simmias.

Is it anything else than the separation of the soul from the body? Do we believe that death is this, namely, that the body comes to be separated by itself apart from the soul, and the soul comes to be separated by itself apart from the body? Is death anything else than that?

No, that is what it is, he said.

Consider then, my good sir, whether you share my opinion, for this will lead us to a better knowledge of what we are investigating. Do you think it is the part of a philosopher to be concerned with such so-called pleasures as those of food and drink?

d

By no means.

What about the pleasures of sex?

Not at all.

What of the other pleasures concerned with the service of the body? Do you think such a man prizes them greatly, the acquisition of distinguished clothes and shoes and the other bodily ornaments? Do you think he values these or despises them, except insofar as one cannot do without them?

e

I think the true philosopher despises them.

Do you not think, he said, that in general such a man's concern is not with the body but that, as far as he can, he turns away from the body towards the soul?

I do.

65   So in the first place, such things show clearly that the philosopher more than other men frees the soul from association with the body as much as possible?

Apparently.

A man who finds no pleasure in such things and has no part in them is thought by the majority not to deserve to live and to be close to death; the man, that is, who does not care for the pleasures of the body.

What you say is certainly true.

Then what about the actual acquiring of knowledge? Is the body an obstacle when one associates with it in the search for knowledge? I

b   mean, for example, do men find any truth in sight or hearing, or are not even the poets forever telling us that we do not see or hear anything accurately, and surely if those two physical senses are not clear or precise, our other senses can hardly be accurate, as they are all inferior to these. Do you not think so?

I certainly do, he said.

When then, he asked, does the soul grasp the truth? For whenever it attempts to examine anything with the body, it is clearly deceived by it.

c   True.

Is it not in reasoning if anywhere that any reality becomes clear to the soul?

Yes.

And indeed the soul reasons best when none of these senses troubles it, neither hearing nor sight, nor pain nor pleasure, but when it is most by itself, taking leave of the body and as far as possible having no contact or association with it in its search for reality.

That is so.

d   And it is then that the soul of the philosopher most disdains the body, flees from it and seeks to be by itself?

It appears so.

What about the following, Simmias? Do we say that there is such a thing as the Just itself, or not?

We do say so, by Zeus.

And the Beautiful, and the Good?

Of course.

And have you ever seen any of these things with your eyes?

In no way, he said.

Or have you ever grasped them with any of your bodily senses? I am speaking of all things such as Bigness, Health, Strength, and, in a word, the reality of all other things, that which each of them essentially is. Is what is most true in them contemplated through the body, or is this the position: Whoever of us prepares himself best and most accurately to grasp that thing itself which he is investigating will come closest to the knowledge of it? e

Obviously.

Then he will do this most perfectly who approaches the object with thought alone, without associating any sight with his thought, or dragging in any sense perception with his reasoning, but who, using pure thought alone, tries to track down each reality pure and by itself, freeing himself as far as possible from eyes and ears and, in a word, from the whole body, because the body confuses the soul and does not allow it to acquire truth and wisdom whenever it is associated with it. Will not that man reach reality, Simmias, if anyone does? 66

What you say, said Simmias, is indeed true.

All these things will necessarily make the true philosophers believe and say to each other something like this: "There is likely to be something such as a path to guide us out of our confusion, because as long as we have a body and our soul is fused with such an evil we shall never adequately attain what we desire, which we affirm to be the truth. The body keeps us busy in a thousand ways because of its need for nurture. Moreover, if certain diseases befall it, they impede our search for the truth. It fills us with wants, desires, fears, all sorts of illusions and much nonsense, so that, as it is said, in truth and in fact no thought of any kind ever comes to us from the body. Only the body and its desires cause war, civil discord, and battles, for all wars are due to the desire to acquire wealth, and it is the body and the care of it, to which we are enslaved, which compel us to acquire wealth, and all this makes us too busy to practice philosophy. Worst of all, if we do get some respite from it and turn to some investigation, everywhere in our investigations the body is present and makes for confusion and fear, so that it prevents us from seeing the truth. b

"It really has been shown to us that, if we are ever to have pure knowledge, we must escape from the body and observe things in themselves with the soul by itself. It seems likely that we shall, only then, when we are dead, attain that which we desire and of which we claim to be lovers, namely, wisdom, as our argument shows, not while we c live; for if it is impossible to attain any pure knowledge with the body, then one of two things is true: either we can never attain knowledge or we can do so after death. Then and not before, the soul is by itself apart from the body. While we live, we shall be closest to knowledge if we refrain as much as possible from association with the body and do not join with it more than we must, if we are not infected with its nature but purify ourselves from it until the god himself frees us. In this way we shall escape the contamination of the body's folly; we shall be likely to be in the company of people of the same kind, and by our own efforts we shall know all that is pure, which is presumably the truth, for it is not permitted to the impure to attain the pure."

Such are the things, Simmias, that all those who love learning in the proper manner must say to one another and believe. Or do you not think so?

I certainly do, Socrates.

And if this is true, my friend, said Socrates, there is good hope that on arriving where I am going, if anywhere, I shall acquire what has been our chief preoccupation in our past life, so that the journey that is now ordered for me is full of good hope, as it is also for any other man who believes that his mind has been prepared and, as it were, purified.

It certainly is, said Simmias.

And does purification not turn out to be what we mentioned in our argument some time ago, namely, to separate the soul as far as possible from the body and accustom it to gather itself and collect itself out of every part of the body and to dwell by itself as far as it can both now and in the future, freed, as it were, from the bonds of the body?

Certainly, he said.

And that freedom and separation of the soul from the body is called death?

That is altogether so.

It is only those who practice philosophy in the right way, we say, who always most want to free the soul; and this release and separation of the soul from the body is the preoccupation of the philosophers?

So it appears.

Therefore, as I said at the beginning, it would be ridiculous for a man to train himself in life to live in a state as close to death as possible, and then to resent it when it comes?

Ridiculous, of course.

In fact, Simmias, he said, those who practice philosophy in the right way are in training for dying and they fear death least of all men.

Consider it from this point of view: If they are altogether estranged from the body and desire to have their soul by itself, would it not be quite absurd for them to be afraid and resentful when this happens? If they did not gladly set out for a place, where, on arrival, they may hope to attain that for which they had yearned during their lifetime, that is, 68 wisdom, and where they would be rid of the presence of that from which they are estranged?

Many men, at the death of their lovers, wives, or sons, were willing to go to the underworld, driven by the hope of seeing there those for whose company they longed, and being with them. Will then a true lover of wisdom, who has a similar hope and knows that he will never find it to any extent except in Hades, be resentful of dying and not gladly undertake the journey thither? One must surely think so, my   b friend, if he is a true philosopher, for he is firmly convinced that he will not find pure knowledge anywhere except there. And if this is so, then, as I said just now, would it not be highly unreasonable for such a man to fear death?

It certainly would, by Zeus, he said.

Then you have sufficient indication, he said, that any man whom you see resenting death was not a lover of wisdom but a lover of the body, and also a lover of wealth or of honors, either or both.   c

It is certainly as you say.

And, Simmias, he said, does not what is called courage belong especially to men of this disposition?

Most certainly.

And the quality of moderation which even the majority call by that name, that is, not to get swept off one's feet by one's passions, but to treat them with disdain and orderliness, is this not suited only to those   d who most of all despise the body and live the life of philosophy?

Necessarily so, he said.

If you are willing to reflect on the courage and moderation of other people, you will find them strange.

In what way, Socrates?

You know that they all consider death a great evil?

Definitely, he said.

And the brave among them face death, when they do, for fear of greater evils?

That is so.

Therefore, it is fear and terror that make all men brave, except the philosophers. Yet it is illogical to be brave through fear and cowardice.

e   It certainly is.

What of the moderate among them? Is their experience not similar? Is it licentiousness of a kind that makes them moderate? We say this is impossible, yet their experience of this simple-minded moderation turns out to be similar: they fear to be deprived of other pleasures which they desire, so they keep away from some pleasures because they are overcome by others. Now to be mastered by pleasure is what they call

69   licentiousness, but what happens to them is that they master certain pleasures because they are mastered by others. This is like what we mentioned just now, that in some way it is a kind of licentiousness that has made them moderate.

That seems likely.

My good Simmias, I fear this is not the right exchange to attain virtue, to exchange pleasures for pleasures, pains for pains, and fears

b   for fears, the greater for the less like coins, but that the only valid currency for which all these things should be exchanged is wisdom. With this we have real courage and moderation and justice and, in a word, true virtue, with wisdom, whether pleasures and fears and all such things be present or absent. When these are exchanged for one another in separation from wisdom, such virtue is only an illusory appearance of virtue; it is in fact fit for slaves, without soundness or truth, whereas, in truth, moderation and courage and justice are a

c   purging away of all such things, and wisdom itself is a kind of cleansing or purification. It is likely that those who established the mystic rites for us were not inferior persons but were speaking in riddles long ago when they said that whoever arrives in the underworld uninitiated and unsanctified will wallow in the mire, whereas he who arrives there purified and initiated will dwell with the gods. There are indeed, as those concerned with the mysteries say, many who carry the thyrsus

d   but the Bacchants are few.[6] These latter are, in my opinion, no other than those who have practiced philosophy in the right way. I have in my life left nothing undone in order to be counted among these as far as possible, as I have been eager to be in every way. Whether my eagerness was right and we accomplished anything we shall, I think, know for certain in a short time, god willing, on arriving yonder.

This is my defense, Simmias and Cebes, that I am likely to be right

e   to leave you and my masters here without resentment or complaint,

---

6. That is, the true worshipers of Dionysus, as opposed to those who only carry the external symbols of his worship.

believing that there, as here, I shall find good masters and good friends. If my defense is more convincing to you than to the Athenian jury, it will be well.

When Socrates finished, Cebes intervened: Socrates, he said, every- thing else you said is excellent, I think, but men find it very hard to believe what you said about the soul. They think that after it has left the body it no longer exists anywhere, but that it is destroyed and dissolved on the day the man dies, as soon as it leaves the body; and that, on leaving it, it is dispersed like breath or smoke, has flown away and gone and is no longer anything anywhere. If indeed it gathered itself together and existed by itself and escaped those evils you were recently enumerating, there would then be much good hope, Socrates, that what you say is true; but to believe this requires a good deal of faith and persuasive argument, to believe that the soul still exists after a man has died and that it still possesses some capability and intelligence.

What you say is true, Cebes, Socrates said, but what shall we do? Do you want to discuss whether this is likely to be true or not?

Personally, said Cebes, I should like to hear your opinion on the subject.

I do not think, said Socrates, that anyone who heard me now, not even a comic poet,[7] could say that I am babbling and discussing things that do not concern me, so we must examine the question thoroughly, if you think we should do so. Let us examine it in some such a manner as this: whether the souls of men who have died exist in the underworld or not. We recall an ancient theory that souls arriving there come from here, and then again that they arrive here and are born here from the dead. If that is true, that the living come back from the dead, then surely our souls must exist there, for they could not come back if they did not exist, and this is a sufficient proof that these things are so if it truly appears that the living never come from any other source than from the dead. If this is not the case we should need another argument.

Quite so, said Cebes.

Do not, he said, confine yourself to humanity if you want to under- stand this more readily, but take all animals and all plants into account, and, in short, for all things which come to be, let us see whether they come to be in this way, that is, from their opposites if they have such, as the beautiful is the opposite of the ugly and the just of the unjust,

7. A veiled reference to Aristophanes, who pilloried Socrates on these grounds in his comic play *Clouds*.

and a thousand other things of the kind. Let us examine whether those
that have an opposite must necessarily come to be from their opposite
and from nowhere else, as, for example, when something comes to be
larger it must necessarily become larger from having been smaller
before.

Yes.

Then if something smaller comes to be, it will come from something
71 larger before, which became smaller?

That is so, he said.

And the weaker comes to be from the stronger, and the swifter from
the slower?

Certainly.

Further, if something worse comes to be, does it not come from the
better, and the juster from the more unjust?

Of course.

So we have sufficiently established that all things come to be in this
way, opposites from opposites?

Certainly.

There is a further point, something such as this, about these opposites:
b   Between each of those pairs of opposites there are two processes: from
the one to the other and then again from the other to the first; between
the larger and the smaller there is increase and decrease, and we call
the one increasing and the other decreasing?

Yes, he said.

And so too there is separation and combination, cooling and heating,
and all such things, even if sometimes we do not have a name for the
process, but in fact it must be everywhere that they come to be from
one another, and that there is a process of becoming from each into
the other?

Assuredly, he said.

c   Well then, is there an opposite to living, as sleeping is the opposite
of being awake?

Quite so, he said.

What is it?

Being dead, he said.

Therefore, if these are opposites, they come to be from one another,
and there are two processes of generation between the two?

Of course.

I will tell you, said Socrates, one of the two pairs I was just talking
about, the pair itself and the two processes, and you will tell me the

other. I mean, to sleep and to be awake; to be awake comes from   d
sleeping, and to sleep comes from being awake. Of the two processes
one is going to sleep, the other is waking up. Do you accept that, or
not?

Certainly.

You tell me in the same way about life and death. Do you not say
that to be dead is the opposite of being alive?

I do.

And they come to be from one another?

Yes.

What comes to be from being alive?

Being dead.

And what comes to be from being dead?

One must agree that it is being alive.

Then, Cebes, living creatures and things come to be from the dead?

So it appears, he said.   e

Then our souls exist in the underworld.

That seems likely.

Then in this case one of the two processes of becoming is clear, for
dying is clear enough, is it not?

It certainly is.

What shall we do then? Shall we not supply the opposite process of
becoming? Is nature to be lame in this case? Or must we provide a
process of becoming opposite to dying?

We surely must.

And what is that?

Coming to life again.

Therefore, he said, if there is such a thing as coming to life again, 72
it would be a process of coming from the dead to the living?

Quite so.

It is agreed between us then that the living come from the dead in
this way no less than the dead from the living, and, if that is so, it seems
to be a sufficient proof that the souls of the dead must be somewhere
whence they can come back again.

I think, Socrates, he said, that this follows from what we have
agreed on.

Consider in this way, Cebes, he said, that, as I think, we were not
wrong to agree. If the two processes of becoming did not always balance b
each other as if they were going round in a circle, but generation
proceeded from one point to its opposite in a straight line and it did

not turn back again to the other opposite or take any turning, do you realize that all things would ultimately be in the same state, be affected in the same way, and cease to become?

How do you mean? he said.

It is not hard to understand what I mean. If, for example, there was such a process as going to sleep, but no corresponding process of waking up, you realize that in the end everything would show the story of
c   Endymion[8] to have no meaning. There would be no point to it because everything would have the same experience as he had and be asleep. And if everything were combined and nothing separated, the saying of Anaxagoras[9] would soon be true, "that all things were mixed together." In the same way, my dear Cebes, if everything that partakes of life were
d   to die and remain in that state and not come to life again, would not everything ultimately have to be dead and nothing alive? Even if the living came from some other source, and all that lived died, how could all things avoid being absorbed in death?

It could not be, Socrates, said Cebes, and I think what you say is altogether true.

I think, Cebes, said he, that this is very definitely the case and that we were not deceived when we agreed on this: Coming to life again
e   in truth exists, the living come to be from the dead, and the souls of the dead exist.

Furthermore, Socrates, Cebes rejoined, such is also the case if that theory is true that you are accustomed to mention frequently, that for us learning is no other than recollection. According to this, we must at some previous time have learned what we now recollect. This is
73   possible only if our soul existed somewhere before it took on this human shape. So according to this theory too, the soul is likely to be something immortal.

Cebes, Simmias interrupted, what are the proofs of this? Remind me, for I do not quite recall them at the moment.

There is one excellent argument, said Cebes, namely that when men are interrogated in the right manner, they always give the right

---

8. Endymion was granted eternal sleep by Zeus.

9. Anaxagoras of Clazomenae was born at the beginning of the fifth century B.C. He came to Athens as a young man and spent most of his life there in the study of natural philosophy. He is quoted later in the dialogue (97c ff.) as claiming that the universe is directed by Mind (Nous). The reference here is to his statement that in the original state of the world all its elements were thoroughly commingled.

answer of their own accord, and they could not do this if they did not possess the knowledge and the right explanation inside them. Then if one shows them a diagram or something else of that kind, this will show most clearly that such is the case.[10]

If this does not convince you, Simmias, said Socrates, see whether you agree if we examine it in some such way as this, for do you doubt that what we call learning is recollection?

It is not that I doubt, said Simmias, but I want to experience the very thing we are discussing, recollection, and from what Cebes undertook to say, I am now remembering and am pretty nearly convinced. Nevertheless, I should like to hear now the way you were intending to explain it.

This way, he said. We surely agree that if anyone recollects anything, he must have known it before.

Quite so, he said.

Do we not also agree that when knowledge comes to mind in this way, it is recollection? What way do I mean? Like this: When a man sees or hears or in some other way perceives one thing and not only knows that thing but also thinks of another thing of which the knowledge is not the same but different, are we not right to say that he recollects the second thing that comes into his mind?

How do you mean?

Things such as this: To know a man is surely a different knowledge from knowing a lyre.

Of course.

Well, you know what happens to lovers: whenever they see a lyre, a garment, or anything else that their beloved is accustomed to use, they know the lyre, and the image of the boy to whom it belongs comes into their mind. This is recollection, just as someone, on seeing Simmias, often recollects Cebes, and there are thousands of other such occurrences.

Thousands indeed, said Simmias.

Is this kind of thing not recollection of a kind, he said, especially so when one experiences it about things that one had forgotten, because one had not seen them for some time? — Quite so.

Further, he said, can a man seeing the picture of a horse or a lyre recollect a man, or seeing a picture of Simmias recollect Cebes? — Certainly.

Or seeing a picture of Simmias, recollect Simmias himself? — He certainly can.

---

10. Cf. *Meno* 81e ff., where Socrates does precisely that.

74   In all these cases the recollection can be occasioned by things that
are similar, but it can also be occasioned by things that are dissimilar?
— It can.

When the recollection is caused by similar things, must one not of
necessity also experience this: to consider whether the similarity to that
which one recollects is deficient in any respect or complete?
— One must.

Consider, he said, whether this is the case: We say that there is
something that is equal. I do not mean a stick equal to a stick or a
stone to a stone, or anything of that kind, but something else beyond
all these, the Equal itself. Shall we say that this exists or not?

b   Indeed we shall, by Zeus, said Simmias, most definitely.

And do we know what this is? — Certainly.

Whence have we acquired the knowledge of it? Is it not from the
things we mentioned just now, from seeing sticks or stones or some
other things that are equal we come to think of that other which is
different from them? Or doesn't it seem to you to be different? Look
at it also this way: Do not equal stones and sticks sometimes, while
remaining the same, appear to one to be equal and to another to be
unequal? — Certainly they do.

c   But what of the equals themselves? Have they ever appeared unequal
to you, or Equality to be Inequality?

Never, Socrates.

These equal things and the Equal itself are therefore not the same?
I do not think they are the same at all, Socrates.

But it is definitely from the equal things, though they are different
from that Equal, that you have derived and grasped the knowledge
of equality?

Very true, Socrates.

Whether it be like them or unlike them?

Certainly.

It makes no difference. As long as the sight of one thing makes you
think of another, whether it be similar or dissimilar, this must of necessity
d   be recollection?

Quite so.

Well then, he said, do we experience something like this in the case
of equal sticks and the other equal objects we just mentioned? Do they
seem to us to be equal in the same sense as what is Equal itself? Is
there some deficiency in their being such as the Equal, or is there not?
A considerable deficiency, he said.

Whenever someone, on seeing something, realizes that that which
he now sees wants to be like some other reality but falls short and   e
cannot be like that other since it is inferior, do we agree that the one
who thinks this must have prior knowledge of that to which he says it
is like, but deficiently so?

Necessarily.

Well, do we also experience this about the equal objects and the
Equal itself, or do we not?

Very definitely.

We must then possess knowledge of the Equal before that time when
we first saw the equal objects and realized that all these objects strive   75
to be like the Equal but are deficient in this.

That is so.

Then surely we also agree that this conception of ours derives from
seeing or touching or some other sense perception, and cannot come
into our mind in any other way, for all these senses, I say, are the same.

They are the same, Socrates, at any rate in respect to that which
our argument wishes to make plain.

Our sense perceptions must surely make us realize that all that we   b
perceive through them is striving to reach that which is Equal but falls
short of it; or how do we express it?

Like that.

Then before we began to see or hear or otherwise perceive, we must
have possessed knowledge of the Equal itself if we were about to refer
our sense perceptions of equal objects to it, and realized that all of
them were eager to be like it, but were inferior.

That follows from what has been said, Socrates.

But we began to see and hear and otherwise perceive right after birth?

Certainly.

We must then have acquired the knowledge of the Equal before this.   c

Yes.

It seems then that we must have possessed it before birth.

It seems so.

Therefore, if we had this knowledge, we knew before birth and
immediately after not only the Equal, but the Greater and the Smaller
and all such things, for our present argument is no more about the
Equal than about the Beautiful itself, the Good itself, the Just, the
Pious, and, as I say, about all those things which we mark with the seal   d
of "what it is," both when we are putting questions and answering them.
So we must have acquired knowledge of them all before we were born.

That is so.

If, having acquired this knowledge in each case, we have not forgotten it, we remain knowing and have knowledge throughout our life, for to know is to acquire knowledge, keep it and not lose it. Do we not call the losing of knowledge forgetting?

e   Most certainly, Socrates, he said.

But, I think, if we acquired this knowledge before birth, then lost it at birth, and then later by the use of our senses in connection with those objects we mentioned, we recovered the knowledge we had before, would not what we call learning be the recovery of our own knowledge, and we are right to call this recollection?

Certainly.

76   It was seen to be possible for someone to see or hear or otherwise perceive something, and by this to be put in mind of something else which he had forgotten and which is related to it by similarity or difference. One of two things follows, as I say: either we were born with the knowledge of it, and all of us know it throughout life, or those who later, we say, are learning, are only recollecting, and learning would be recollection.

That is certainly the case, Socrates.

Which alternative do you choose, Simmias? That we are born with b   this knowledge or that we recollect later the things of which we had knowledge previously?

I have no means of choosing at the moment, Socrates.

Well, can you make this choice? What is your opinion about it? A man who has knowledge would be able to give an account of what he knows, or would he not?

He must certainly be able to do so, Socrates, he said.

And do you think everybody can give an account of the things we were mentioning just now?

I wish they could, said Simmias, but I'm afraid it is much more likely that by this time tomorrow there will be no one left who can do so adequately.

c   So you do not think that everybody has knowledge of those things?

No indeed.

So they recollect what they once learned?

They must.

When did our souls acquire the knowledge of them? Certainly not since we were born as men.

Indeed no.

Before that then?

Yes.

So then, Simmias, our souls also existed apart from the body before they took on human form, and they had intelligence.

Unless we acquire the knowledge at the moment of birth, Socrates, for that time is still left to us.

Quite so, my friend, but at what other time do we lose it? We just   d
now agreed that we are not born with that knowledge. Do we then lose it at the very time we acquire it, or can you mention any other time?

I cannot, Socrates. I did not realize that I was talking nonsense.

So this is our position, Simmias? he said. If those realities we are always talking about exist, the Beautiful and the Good and all that kind of reality, and we refer all the things we perceive to that reality, discovering that it existed before and is ours, and we compare these   e
things with it, then, just as they exist, so our soul must exist before we are born. If these realities do not exist, then this argument is altogether futile. Is this the position, that there is an equal necessity for those realities to exist, and for our souls to exist before we were born? If the former do not exist, neither do the latter?

I do not think, Socrates, said Simmias, that there is any possible doubt that it is equally necessary for both to exist, and it is opportune that our argument comes to the conclusion that our soul exists before   77
we are born, and equally so that reality of which you are now speaking. Nothing is so evident to me personally as that all such things must certainly exist, the Beautiful, the Good, and all those you mentioned just now. I also think that sufficient proof of this has been given.

Then what about Cebes? said Socrates, for we must persuade Cebes also.

He is sufficiently convinced I think, said Simmias, though he is the most difficult of men to persuade by argument, but I believe him to be fully convinced that our soul existed before we were born. I do not   b
think myself, however, that it has been proved that the soul continues to exist after death; the opinion of the majority which Cebes mentioned still stands, that when a man dies his soul is dispersed and this is the end of its existence. What is to prevent the soul coming to be and being constituted from some other source, existing before it enters a human body and then, having done so and departed from it, itself dying and being destroyed?

You are right, Simmias, said Cebes. Half of what needed proof has   c
been proved, namely, that our soul existed before we were born, but

further proof is needed that it exists no less after we have died, if the proof is to be complete.

It has been proved even now, Simmias and Cebes, said Socrates, if you are ready to combine this argument with the one we agreed on before, that every living thing must come from the dead. If the soul
d   exists before, it must, as it comes to life and birth, come from nowhere else than death and being dead, so how could it avoid existing after death since it must be born again? What you speak of has then even now been proved. However, I think you and Simmias would like to discuss the argument more fully. You seem to have this childish fear that the wind would really dissolve and scatter the soul, as it leaves the
e   body, especially if one happens to die in a high wind and not in calm weather.

Cebes laughed and said: Assuming that we were afraid, Socrates, try to change our minds, or rather do not assume that we are afraid, but perhaps there is a child in us who has these fears; try to persuade him not to fear death like a bogey.

You should, said Socrates, sing a charm over him every day until you have charmed away his fears.

78   Where shall we find a good charmer for these fears, Socrates, he said, now that you are leaving us?

Greece is a large country, Cebes, he said, and there are good men in it; the tribes of foreigners are also numerous. You should search for such a charmer among them all, sparing neither trouble nor expense, for there is nothing on which you could spend your money to greater advantage. You must also search among yourselves, for you might not easily find people who could do this better than yourselves.

b   That shall be done, said Cebes, but let us, if it pleases you, go back to the argument where we left it.

Of course it pleases me.

Splendid, he said.

We must then ask ourselves something like this: What kind of thing is likely to be scattered? On behalf of what kind of thing should one fear this, and for what kind of thing should one not fear it? We should then examine to which class the soul belongs, and as a result either fear for the soul or be of good cheer.

What you say is true.

c   Is not anything that is composite and a compound by nature liable to be split up into its component parts, and only that which is noncomposite, if anything, is not likely to be split up?

I think that is the case, said Cebes.

Are not the things that always remain the same and in the same state most likely not to be composite, whereas those that vary from one time to another and are never the same are composite?

I think that is so.

Let us then return to those same things with which we were dealing earlier, to that reality of whose existence we are giving an account in   d
our questions and answers; are they ever the same and in the same state, or do they vary from one time to another; can the Equal itself, the Beautiful itself, each thing in itself, the real, ever be affected by any change whatever? Or does each of them that really is, being uniform by itself, remain the same and never in any way tolerate any change whatever?

It must remain the same, said Cebes, and in the same state, Socrates.

What of the many beautiful particulars, be they men, horses, clothes,   e
or other such things, or the many equal particulars, and all those which bear the same name as those others? Do they remain the same or, in total contrast to those other realities, one might say, never in any way remain the same as themselves or in relation to each other?

The latter is the case; they are never in the same state.

These latter you could touch and see and perceive with the other   79
senses, but those that always remain the same can be grasped only by the reasoning power of the mind? They are not seen but are invisible?

That is altogether true, he said.

Do you then want us to assume two kinds of existences, the visible and the invisible?

Let us assume this.

And the invisible always remains the same, whereas the visible never does?

Let us assume that too.

Now one part of ourselves is the body, another part is the soul?   b
Quite so.

To which class of existence do we say the body is more alike and akin?

To the visible, as anyone can see.

What about the soul? Is it visible or invisible?

It is not visible to men, Socrates, he said.

Well, we meant visible and invisible to human eyes. Or do you think we meant to some others?

To human eyes.

Then what do we say about the soul? Is it visible or not visible?

Not visible.

So it is invisible? — Yes.

c So the soul is more like the invisible than the body, and the body more like the visible? — Without any doubt, Socrates.

Haven't we also said some time ago that when the soul makes use of the body to investigate something, be it through hearing or seeing or some other sense—for to investigate something through the body is to do it through the senses—it is dragged by the body to the things that are never the same, and the soul itself strays and is confused and dizzy, as if it were drunk, insofar as it is in contact with that kind of thing?

Certainly.

d But when the soul investigates by itself it passes into the realm of what is pure, ever existing, immortal and unchanging, and being akin to this, it always stays with it whenever it is by itself and can do so; it ceases to stray and remains in the same state as it is in touch with things of the same kind, and its experience then is what is called wisdom?

Altogether well said and very true, Socrates, he said.

e Judging from what we have said before and what we are saying now, to which of these two kinds do you think that the soul is more alike and more akin?

I think, Socrates, he said, that on this line of argument any man, even the dullest, would agree that the soul is altogether more like that which always exists in the same state rather than like that which does not.

What of the body?

That is like the other.

80 Look at it also this way: When the soul and the body are together, nature orders the one to be subject and to be ruled, and the other to rule and be master. Then again, which do you think is like the divine and which like the mortal? Do you not think that the nature of the divine is to rule and to lead, whereas it is that of the mortal to be ruled and be subject?

I do.

Which does the soul resemble?

Obviously, Socrates, the soul resembles the divine, and the body resembles the mortal.

Consider then, Cebes, whether it follows from all that has been said

b that the soul is most like the divine, deathless, intelligible, uniform, indissoluble, always the same as itself, whereas the body is most like that which is human, mortal, multiform, unintelligible, soluble, and never consistently the same. Have we anything else to say to show, my dear Cebes, that this is not the case?

We have not.

Well then, that being so, is it not natural for the body to dissolve easily, and for the soul to be altogether indissoluble, or nearly so?

Of course.   c

You realize, he said, that when a man dies, the visible part, the body, which exists in the visible world, and which we call the corpse, whose natural lot it would be to dissolve, fall apart, and be blown away, does not immediately suffer any of these things but remains for a fair time, in fact, quite a long time if the man dies with his body in a suitable condition and at a favorable season? If the body is emaciated or embalmed, as in Egypt, it remains almost whole for a remarkable length of time, and even if the body decays, some parts of it, namely bones   d and sinews and the like, are nevertheless, one might say, deathless. Is that not so? — Yes.

Will the soul, the invisible part which makes its way to a region of the same kind, noble and pure and invisible, to Hades in fact, to the good and wise god whither, god willing, my soul must soon be going — will the soul, being of this kind and nature, be scattered and destroyed on leaving the body, as the majority of men say? Far from it, my dear Cebes and Simmias, but what happens is much more like this: If it is   e pure when it leaves the body and drags nothing bodily with it, as it had no willing association with the body in life, but avoided it and gathered itself together by itself and always practiced this, which is no other than practicing philosophy in the right way, in fact, training to die easily.   81 Or is this not training for death?

It surely is.

A soul in this state makes its way to the invisible, which is like itself, the divine and immortal and wise, and arriving there it can be happy, having rid itself of confusion, ignorance, fear, violent desires, and the other human ills and, as is said of the initiates, truly spend the rest of time with the gods. Shall we say this, Cebes, or something different?

This, by Zeus, said Cebes.

But I think that if the soul is polluted and impure when it leaves   b the body, having always been associated with it and served it, bewitched by physical desires and pleasures to the point at which nothing seems to exist for it but the physical, which one can touch and see or eat and drink or make use of for sexual enjoyment, and if that soul is accustomed to hate and fear and avoid that which is dim and invisible to the eyes but intelligible and to be grasped by philosophy—do you think such a soul will escape pure and by itself?

Impossible, he said.   c

It is no doubt permeated by the physical, which constant intercourse and association with the body, as well as considerable practice, has caused to become ingrained in it?

Quite so.

We must believe, my friend, that this bodily element is heavy, ponderous, earthy, and visible. Through it, such a soul has become heavy and is dragged back to the visible region in fear of the unseen and of
d Hades. It wanders, as we are told, around graves and monuments, where shadowy phantoms, images that such souls produce, have been seen, souls that have not been freed and purified but share in the visible, and are therefore seen.

That is likely, Socrates.

It is indeed, Cebes. Moreover, these are not the souls of good but of inferior men, which are forced to wander there, paying the penalty
e for their previous bad upbringing. They wander until their longing for that which accompanies them, the physical, again imprisons them in a body, and they are then, as is likely, bound to such characters as they have practiced in their life.

What kind of characters do you say these are, Socrates?

Those, for example, who have carelessly practiced gluttony, violence, and drunkenness are likely to join a company of donkeys or of similar
82 animals. Do you not think so?

Very likely.

Those who have esteemed injustice highly, and tyranny and plunder, will join the tribes of wolves and hawks and kites, or where else shall we say that they go?

Certainly to those, said Cebes.

And clearly, the destination of the others will conform to the way in which they have behaved?

Clearly, of course.

The happiest of these, who will also have the best destination, are
b those who have practiced popular and social virtue, which they call moderation and justice and which was developed by habit and practice, without philosophy or understanding?

How are they the happiest?

Because it is likely that they will again join a social and gentle group, either of bees or wasps or ants, and then again the same kind of human group, and so be moderate men.

That is likely.

No one may join the company of the gods who has not practiced
c philosophy and is not completely pure when he departs from life, no

one but the lover of learning. It is for this reason, my friends Simmias and Cebes, that those who practice philosophy in the right way keep away from all bodily passions, master them and do not surrender themselves to them; it is not at all for fear of wasting their substance and of poverty, which the majority and the money-lovers fear, nor for fear of dishonor and ill repute, like the ambitious and lovers of honors, that they keep away from them.

That would not be natural for them, Socrates, said Cebes.

By Zeus, no, he said. Those who care for their own soul and do not live for the service of their body dismiss all these things. They do not travel the same road as those who do not know where they are going but, believing that nothing should be done contrary to philosophy and their deliverance and purification, they turn to this and follow wherever philosophy leads.

How so, Socrates?

I will tell you, he said. The lovers of learning know that when philosophy gets hold of their soul, it is imprisoned in and clinging to the body, and that it is forced to examine other things through it as through a cage and not by itself, and that it wallows in every kind of ignorance. Philosophy sees that the worst feature of this imprisonment is that it is due to desires, so that the prisoner himself is contributing to his own incarceration most of all. As I say, the lovers of learning know that philosophy gets hold of their soul when it is in that state, then gently encourages it and tries to free it by showing them that investigation through the eyes is full of deceit, as is that through the ears and the other senses. Philosophy then persuades the soul to withdraw from the senses insofar as it is not compelled to use them and bids the soul to gather itself together by itself, to trust only itself and whatever reality, existing by itself, the soul by itself understands, and not to consider as true whatever it examines by other means, for this is different in different circumstances and is sensible and visible, whereas what the soul itself sees is intelligible and invisible. The soul of the true philosopher thinks that this deliverance must not be opposed and so keeps away from pleasures and desires and pains as far as he can; he reflects that violent pleasure or pain or passion does not cause merely such evils as one might expect, such as one suffers when one has been sick or extravagant through desire, but the greatest and most extreme evil, though one does not reflect on this.

What is that, Socrates? asked Cebes.

That the soul of every man, when it feels violent pleasure or pain in connection with some object, inevitably believes at the same time that what causes such feelings must be very clear and very true, which it is not. Such objects are mostly visible, are they not?

Certainly.

d   And doesn't such an experience tie the soul to the body most completely?

How so?

Because every pleasure or pain provides, as it were, another nail to rivet the soul to the body and to weld them together. It makes the soul corporeal, so that it believes that truth is what the body says it is. As it shares the beliefs and delights of the body, I think it inevitably comes to share its ways and manner of life and is unable ever to reach Hades in a pure state; it is always full of body when it departs, so that e   it soon falls back into another body and grows with it as if it had been sewn into it. Because of this, it can have no part in the company of the divine, the pure and uniform.

What you say is very true, Socrates, said Cebes.

This is why genuine lovers of learning are moderate and brave, or do you think it is for the reasons the majority says they are?

84   I certainly do not.

Indeed no. This is how the soul of a philosopher would reason: It would not think that while philosophy must free it, it should while being freed surrender itself to pleasures and pains and imprison itself again, thus laboring in vain like Penelope at her web. The soul of the philosopher achieves a calm from such emotions; it follows reason and ever stays with it contemplating the true, the divine, which is not the b   object of opinion. Nurtured by this, it believes that one should live in this manner as long as one is alive and, after death, arrive at what is akin and of the same kind, and escape from human evils. After such nurture there is no danger, Simmias and Cebes, that one should fear that, on parting from the body, the soul would be scattered and dissipated by the winds and no longer be anything anywhere.

c   When Socrates finished speaking there was a long silence. He appeared to be concentrating on what had been said, and so were most of us. But Cebes and Simmias were whispering to each other. Socrates observed them and questioned them. Come, he said, do you think there is something lacking in my argument? There are still many doubtful points and many objections for anyone who wants a thorough discussion of these matters. If you are discussing some other subject, I have nothing to say, but if you have some difficulty about this one, do not hesitate to speak for yourselves and expound it if you think the argument

could be improved, and if you think you will do better, take me along   d
with you in the discussion.

I will tell you the truth, Socrates, said Simmias. Both of us have
been in difficulty for some time, and each of us has been urging the
other to question you because we wanted to hear what you would say,
but we hesitated to bother you, lest it be displeasing to you in your
present misfortune.

When Socrates heard this he laughed quietly and said: "Really,
Simmias, it would be hard for me to persuade other people that I do   e
not consider my present fate a misfortune if I cannot persuade even
you, and you are afraid that it is more difficult to deal with me than
before. You seem to think me inferior to the swans in prophecy. They
sing before too, but when they realize that they must die they sing most
and most beautifully, as they rejoice that they are about to depart to   85
join the god whose servants they are. But men, because of their own
fear of death, tell lies about the swans and say that they lament their
death and sing in sorrow. They do not reflect that no bird sings when
it is hungry or cold or suffers in any other way, neither the nightingale
nor the swallow nor the hoopoe, though they do say that these sing
laments when in pain. Nor do the swans, but I believe that as they
belong to Apollo, they are prophetic, have knowledge of the future,   b
and sing of the blessings of the underworld, sing and rejoice on that
day beyond what they did before. As I believe myself to be a fellow
servant with the swans and dedicated to the same god, and have received
from my master a gift of prophecy not inferior to theirs, I am no more
despondent than they on leaving life. Therefore, you must speak and
ask whatever you want as long as the authorities allow it."

Well spoken, said Simmias. I will tell you my difficulty, and then
Cebes will say why he does not accept what was said. I believe, as   c
perhaps you do, that precise knowledge on that subject is impossible
or extremely difficult in our present life, but that it surely shows a very
poor spirit not to examine thoroughly what is said about it, and to desist
before one is exhausted by an all-around investigation. One should
achieve one of these things: learn the truth about these things or find
it for oneself, or, if that is impossible, adopt the best and most irrefutable   d
of men's theories, and, borne upon this, sail through the dangers of
life as upon a raft, unless someone should make that journey safer and
less risky upon a firmer vessel of some divine doctrine. So even now,
since you have said what you did, I will feel no shame at asking questions,
and I will not blame myself in the future because I did not say what I

think. As I examine what we said, both by myself and with Cebes, it does not seem to be adequate.

e   Said Socrates: "You may well be right, my friend, but tell me how it is inadequate."

In this way, as it seems to me, he said: "One might make the same argument about harmony, lyre and strings, that a harmony is something
86   invisible, without body, beautiful and divine in the attuned lyre, whereas the lyre itself and its strings are physical, bodily, composite, earthy, and akin to what is mortal. Then if someone breaks the lyre, cuts or breaks the strings and then insists, using the same argument as you, that the harmony must still exist and is not destroyed because it would be impossible for the lyre and the strings, which are mortal, still to exist when the strings are broken, and for the harmony, which is akin and
b   of the same nature as the divine and immortal, to be destroyed before that which is mortal; he would say that the harmony itself still must exist and that the wood and the strings must rot before the harmony can suffer. And indeed, Socrates, I think you must have this in mind, that we really do suppose the soul to be something of this kind; as the body is stretched and held together by the hot and the cold, the dry
c   and the moist, and other such things, and our soul is a mixture and harmony of those things when they are mixed with each other rightly and in due measure. If then the soul is a kind of harmony or attunement, clearly, when our body is relaxed or stretched without due measure by diseases and other evils, the soul must immediately be destroyed, even if it be most divine, as are the other harmonies found in music and all the works of artists, and the remains of each body last for a long time
d   until they rot or are burned. Consider what we shall say in answer to one who deems the soul to be a mixture of bodily elements and to be the first to perish in the process we call death."

Socrates looked at us keenly, as was his habit, smiled, and said: "What Simmias says is quite fair. If one of you is more resourceful than I am, why did he not answer him, for he seems to have handled the argument competently. However, I think that before we answer him,
e   we should hear Cebes' objection, in order that we may have time to deliberate on an answer. When we have heard him we should either agree with them, if we think them in tune with us or, if not, defend our own argument. Come then, Cebes. What is troubling you?"

87   I tell you, said Cebes, the argument seems to me to be at the same point as before and open to the same objection. I do not deny that it has been very elegantly and, if it is not offensive to say so, sufficiently

proved that our soul existed before it took on this present form, but I do not believe the same applies to its existing somewhere after our death. Not that I agree with Simmias' objection that the soul is not stronger and much more lasting than the body, for I think it is superior in all these respects. "Why then," the argument might say, "are you still unconvinced? Since you see that when the man dies, the weaker part continues to exist, do you not think that the more lasting part must   b
be preserved during that time?" On this point consider whether what I say makes sense.

Like Simmias, I too need an image, for I think this argument is much as if one said at the death of an old weaver that the man had not perished but was safe and sound somewhere, and offered as proof the fact that the cloak the old man had woven himself and was wearing   c
was still sound and had not perished. If one was not convinced, he would be asked whether a man lasts longer than a cloak which is in use and being worn, and if the answer was that a man lasts much longer, this would be taken as proof that the man was definitely safe and sound, since the more temporary thing had not perished. But, Simmias, I do not think that is so, for consider what I say. Anybody could see that the man who said this was talking nonsense. That weaver had woven and worn out many such cloaks. He perished after many   d
of them, but before the last. That does not mean that a man is inferior and weaker than a cloak. The image illustrates, I think, the relationship of the soul to the body, and anyone who says the same thing about them would appear to me to be talking sense, that the soul lasts a long time while the body is weaker and more short-lived. He might say that each soul wears out many bodies, especially if it lives many years. If the body were in a state of flux and perished while the man was still alive, and the soul wove afresh the body that is worn out, yet it would   e
be inevitable that whenever the soul perished it would be wearing the last body it wove and perish only before this last. Then when the soul perished, the body would show the weakness of its nature by soon decaying and disappearing. So we cannot trust this argument and be confident that our soul continues to exist somewhere after our death.   88
For, if one were to concede, even more than you do, to a man using that argument, if one were to grant him not only that the soul exists in the time before we are born, but that there is no reason why the soul of some should not exist and continue to exist after our death, and thus frequently be born and die in turn; if one were to grant him that the soul's nature is so strong that it can survive many bodies, but if,

having granted all this, one does not further agree that the soul is not damaged by its many births and is not, in the end, altogether destroyed
b in one of those deaths, he might say that no one knows which death and dissolution of the body brings about the destruction of the soul, since not one of us can be aware of this. And in that case, any man who faces death with confidence is foolish, unless he can prove that the soul is altogether immortal. If he cannot, a man about to die must of necessity always fear for his soul, lest the present separation of the soul from the body bring about the complete destruction of the soul.

c   When we heard what they said we were all depressed, as we told each other afterwards. We had been quite convinced by the previous argument, and they seemed to confuse us again, and to drive us to doubt not only what had already been said but also what was going to be said, lest we be worthless as critics or the subject itself admitted of no certainty.

ECHECRATES: By the gods, Phaedo, you have my sympathy, for as I
d listen to you now I find myself saying to myself: "What argument shall we trust, now that that of Socrates, which was extremely convincing, has fallen into discredit?" The statement that the soul is some kind of harmony has a remarkable hold on me, now and always, and when it was mentioned it reminded me that I had myself previously thought so. And now I am again quite in need, as if from the beginning, of some other argument to convince me that the soul does not die along with the man. Tell me then, by Zeus, how Socrates tackled the argument.
e Was he obviously distressed, as you say you people were, or was he not, but quietly came to the rescue of his argument, and did he do so satisfactorily or inadequately? Tell us everything as precisely as you can.

PHAEDO: I have certainly often admired Socrates, Echecrates, but
89 never more than on this occasion. That he had a reply was perhaps not strange. What I wondered at most in him was the pleasant, kind, and admiring way he received the young men's argument, and how sharply he was aware of the effect the discussion had on us, and then how well he healed our distress and, as it were, recalled us from our flight and defeat and turned us around to join him in the examination of their argument.

ECHECRATES: How did he do this?

PHAEDO: I will tell you. I happened to be sitting on his right by the
b couch on a low stool, so that he was sitting well above me. He stroked my head and pressed the hair on the back of my neck, for he was in

the habit of playing with my hair at times. "Tomorrow, Phaedo," he said, "you will probably cut this beautiful hair."

Likely enough, Socrates, I said.

Not if you take my advice, he said.

Why not? said I.

It is today, he said, that I shall cut my hair and you yours, if our argument dies on us, and we cannot revive it. If I were you, and the   c argument escaped me, I would take an oath, as the Argives did, not to let my hair grow before I fought again and defeated the argument of Simmias and Cebes.

But, I said, they say that not even Heracles could fight two people.

Then call on me as your Iolaus, as long as the daylight lasts.

I shall call on you, but in this case as Iolaus calling on Heracles.

It makes no difference, he said, but first there is a certain experience we must be careful to avoid.

What is that? I asked.

That we should not become misologues, as people become misan-   d thropes. There is no greater evil one can suffer than to hate reasonable discourse. Misology and misanthropy arise in the same way. Misanthropy comes when a man without knowledge or skill has placed great trust in someone and believes him to be altogether truthful, sound, and trustworthy; then, a short time afterwards he finds him to be wicked and unreliable, and then this happens in another case; when one has frequently had that experience, especially with those whom one believed   e to be one's closest friends, then, in the end, after many such blows, one comes to hate all men and to believe that no one is sound in any way at all. Have you not seen this happen?

I surely have, I said.

This is a shameful state of affairs, he said, and obviously due to an attempt to have human relations without any skill in human affairs, for such skill would lead one to believe, what is in fact true, that the very good and the very wicked are both quite rare, and that most men are   90 between those extremes.

How do you mean? said I.

The same as with the very tall and the very short, he said. Do you think anything is rarer than to find an extremely tall man or an extremely short one? Or a dog or anything else whatever? Or again, one extremely swift or extremely slow, ugly or beautiful, white or black? Are you not aware that in all those cases the most extreme at either end are rare and few, but those in between are many and plentiful?

Certainly, I said.

b   Therefore, he said, if a contest of wickedness were established, there too the winners, you think, would be very few?

That is likely, said I.

Likely indeed, he said, but arguments are not like men in this particular. I was merely following your lead just now. The similarity lies rather in this: It is as when one who lacks skill in arguments puts his trust in an argument as being true, then shortly afterwards believes it to be false—as sometimes it is and sometimes it is not—and so with another argument and then another. You know how those in particular

c   who spend their time studying contradiction in the end believe themselves to have become very wise and that they alone have understood that there is no soundness or reliability in any object or in any argument, but that all that exists simply fluctuates up and down as if it were in the Euripus[11] and does not remain in the same place for any time at all.

What you say, I said, is certainly true.

It would be pitiable, Phaedo, he said, when there is a true and reliable argument and one that can be understood, if a man who has

d   dealt with such arguments as appear at one time true, at another time untrue, should not blame himself or his own lack of skill but, because of his distress, in the end gladly shift the blame away from himself to the arguments, and spend the rest of his life hating and reviling reasoned discussion and so be deprived of truth and knowledge of reality.

Yes, by Zeus, I said, that would be pitiable indeed.

e   This then is the first thing we should guard against, he said. We should not allow into our minds the conviction that argumentation has nothing sound about it; much rather we should believe that it is we who are not yet sound and that we must take courage and be eager to

91   attain soundness, you and the others for the sake of your whole life still to come, and I for the sake of death itself. I am in danger at this moment of not having a philosophical attitude about this, but like those who are quite uneducated, I am eager to get the better of you in argument, for the uneducated, when they engage in argument about anything, give no thought to the truth about the subject of discussion but are only eager that those present will accept the position they have set forth. I differ from them only to this extent: I shall not be eager to get the agreement of those present that what I say is true, except incidentally,

---

11. The Euripus is the straits between the island of Euboea and Boeotia on the Greek mainland; its currents were both violent and variable.

but I shall be very eager that I should myself be thoroughly convinced
that things are so. For I am thinking—see in how contentious a spirit—   b
that if what I say is true, it is a fine thing to be convinced; if, on the
other hand, nothing exists after death, at least for this time before I die
I shall distress those present less with lamentations, and my folly will
not continue to exist along with me—that would be a bad thing—but
will come to an end in a short time. Thus prepared, Simmias and
Cebes, he said, I come to deal with your argument. If you will take my
advice, you will give but little thought to Socrates but much more to   c
the truth. If you think that what I say is true, agree with me; if not,
oppose it with every argument and take care that in my eagerness I do
not deceive myself and you and, like a bee, leave my sting in you when
I go.

We must proceed, he said, and first remind me of what you said if
I do not appear to remember it. Simmias, as I believe, is in doubt and
fear that the soul, though it is more divine and beautiful than the body,   d
yet predeceases it, being a kind of harmony. Cebes, I thought, agrees
with me that the soul lasts much longer than the body, but that no one
knows whether the soul often wears out many bodies and then, on
leaving its last body, is now itself destroyed. This then is death, the
destruction of the soul, since the body is always being destroyed. Are
these the questions, Simmias and Cebes, which we must investigate?

They both agreed that they were.   e

Do you then, he asked, reject all our previous statements, or some
but not others?

Some, they both said, but not others.

What, he said, about the statements we made that learning is recollection and that, if this was so, our soul must of necessity exist elsewhere   92
before us, before it was imprisoned in the body?

For myself, said Cebes, I was wonderfully convinced by it at the
time and I stand by it now also, more than by any other statement.

That, said Simmias, is also my position, and I should be very surprised
if I ever changed my opinion about this.

But you must change your opinion, my Theban friend, said Socrates,
if you still believe that a harmony is a composite thing, and that the soul
is a kind of harmony of the elements of the body in a state of tension, for
surely you will not allow yourself to maintain that a composite harmony   b
existed before those elements from which it had to be composed, or
would you?

Never, Socrates, he said.

Do you realize, he said, that this is what you are in fact saying when you state that the soul exists before it takes on the form and body of a man and that it is composed of elements which do not yet exist? A harmony is not like that to which you compare it; the lyre and the strings and the notes, though still unharmonized, exist; the harmony is composed last of all, and is the first to be destroyed. How will you harmonize this statement with your former one?

In no way, said Simmias.

And surely, he said, a statement about harmony should do so more than any other.

It should, said Simmias.

So your statement is inconsistent? Consider which of your statements you prefer, that learning is recollection or that the soul is a harmony.

I much prefer the former, Socrates. I adopted the latter without proof, because of a certain probability and plausibility, which is why it appeals to most men. I know that arguments of which the proof is based on probability are pretentious and, if one does not guard against them, they certainly deceive one, in geometry and everything else. The theory of recollection and learning, however, was based on an assumption worthy of acceptance, for our soul was said to exist also before it came into the body, just as the reality does that is of the kind that we qualify by the words "what it is," and I convinced myself that I was quite correct to accept it. Therefore, I cannot accept the theory that the soul is a harmony either from myself or anyone else.

What of this, Simmias? Do you think it natural for a harmony, or any other composite, to be in a different state from that of the elements of which it is composed?

Not at all, said Simmias.

Nor, as I think, can it act or be acted upon in a different way than its elements?

He agreed.

One must therefore suppose that a harmony does not direct its components, but is directed by them.

He accepted this.

A harmony is therefore far from making a movement, or uttering a sound, or doing anything else, in a manner contrary to that of its parts.

Far from it indeed, he said.

Does not the nature of each harmony depend on the way it has been harmonized?

I do not understand, he said.

Will it not, if it is more and more fully harmonized, be more and   b
more fully a harmony, and if it is less and less fully harmonized, it will
be less and less fully a harmony?

Certainly.

Can this be true about the soul, that one soul is more and more
fully a soul than another, or is less and less fully a soul, even to the
smallest extent?

Not in any way.

Come now, by Zeus, he said. One soul is said to have intelligence
and virtue and to be good, another to have folly and wickedness and   c
to be bad. Are those things truly said?

They certainly are.

What will someone who holds the theory that the soul is a harmony
say that those things are which reside in the soul, that is, virtue and
wickedness? Are these some other harmony and disharmony? That the
good soul is harmonized and, being a harmony, has within itself another
harmony, whereas the evil soul is both itself a lack of harmony and has
no other within itself?

I don't know what to say, said Simmias, but one who holds that
assumption must obviously say something of that kind.

We have previously agreed, he said, that one soul is not more and   d
not less a soul than another, and this means that one harmony is not
more and more fully, or less and less fully, a harmony than another.
Is that not so?

Certainly.

Now that which is no more and no less a harmony is not more or
less harmonized. Is that so?

It is.

Can that which is neither more nor less harmonized partake more
or less of harmony, or does it do so equally?

Equally.

Then if a soul is neither more nor less a soul than another, it has   e
been harmonized to the same extent?

This is so.

If that is so, it would have no greater share of disharmony or of
harmony?

It would not.

That being the case, could one soul have more wickedness or virtue
than another, if wickedness is disharmony and virtue harmony?

It could not.

94   But rather, Simmias, according to correct reasoning, no soul, if it is a harmony, will have any share of wickedness, for harmony is surely altogether this very thing, harmony, and would never share in disharmony.

It certainly would not.

Nor would a soul, being altogether this very thing, a soul, share in wickedness?

How could it, in view of what has been said?

So it follows from this argument that all the souls of all living creatures will be equally good, if souls are by nature equally this very thing, souls.

I think so, Socrates.

b   Does our argument seem right, he said, and does it seem that it should have come to this, if the hypothesis that the soul is a harmony was correct?

Not in any way, he said.

Further, of all the parts of a man, can you mention any other part that rules him than his soul, especially if it is a wise soul?

I cannot.

Does it do so by following the affections of the body or by opposing them? I mean, for example, that when the body is hot and thirsty the soul draws him to the opposite, to not drinking; when the body is hungry, to not eating, and we see a thousand other examples of the

c   soul opposing the affections of the body. Is that not so?

It certainly is.

On the other hand, we previously agreed that if the soul were a harmony, it would never be out of tune with the stress and relaxation and the striking of the strings or anything else done to its composing elements, but that it would follow and never direct them?

We did so agree, of course.

Well, does it now appear to do quite the opposite, ruling over all

d   the elements of which one says it is composed, opposing nearly all of them throughout life, directing all their ways, inflicting harsh and painful punishment on them, at times in physical culture and medicine, at other times more gently by threats and exhortations, holding converse with desires and passions and fears as if it were one thing talking to a different one, as Homer wrote somewhere in the *Odyssey* where he says that Odysseus "struck his breast and rebuked his heart saying, 'Endure, my heart, you have endured worse than this' "?[12]

---

12. *Odyssey* xx.17–18.

Do you think that when he composed this the poet thought that his   e
soul was a harmony, a thing to be directed by the affections of the
body? Did he not rather regard it as ruling over them and mastering
them, itself a much more divine thing than a harmony?

Yes, by Zeus, I think so, Socrates.

Therefore, my good friend, it is quite wrong for us to say that the   95
soul is a harmony, and in saying so we would disagree both with the
divine poet Homer and with ourselves.

That is so, he said.

Very well, said Socrates. Harmonia of Thebes seems somehow reasonably propitious to us. How and by what argument, my dear Cebes,
can we propitiate Cadmus?[13]

I think, Cebes said, that you will find a way. You dealt with the
argument about harmony in a manner that was quite astonishing to
me. When Simmias was speaking of his difficulties I was very much   b
wondering whether anyone would be able to deal with his argument,
and I was quite dumbfounded when right away he could not resist your
argument's first onslaught. I should not wonder, therefore, if that of
Cadmus suffered the same fate.

My good sir, said Socrates, do not boast, lest some malign influence
upset the argument we are about to make. However, we leave that to
the care of the god, but let us come to grips with it in the Homeric
fashion, to see if there is anything in what you say. The sum of your
problem is this: You consider that the soul must be proved to be
immortal and indestructible before a philosopher on the point of death,   c
who is confident that he will fare much better in the underworld than
if he had led any other kind of life, can avoid being foolish and simple-
minded in this confidence. To prove that the soul is strong, that it is
divine, that it existed before we were born as men, all this, you say,
does not show the soul to be immortal but only long-lasting. That it
existed for a very long time before, that it knew much and acted much,
makes it no more immortal because of that; indeed, its very entering   d
into a human body was the beginning of its destruction, like a disease;
it would live that life in distress and would in the end be destroyed in
what we call death. You say it makes no difference whether it enters a
body once or many times as far as the fear of each of us is concerned,
for it is natural for a man who is no fool to be afraid, if he does not

---

13. Harmonia was in legend the wife of Cadmus, the founder of Thebes.
Socrates' punning joke is simply that, having dealt with Harmonia (harmony),
we must now deal with Cadmus (i.e., Cebes, the other Theban).

know and cannot prove that the soul is immortal. This, I think, is what you maintain, Cebes; I deliberately repeat it often, in order that no point may escape us, and that you may add or subtract something if you wish.

And Cebes said: "There is nothing that I want to add or subtract at the moment. That is what I say."

Socrates paused for a long time, deep in thought. He then said: "This is no unimportant problem that you raise, Cebes, for it requires a thorough investigation of the cause of generation and destruction. I will, if you wish, give you an account of my experience in these matters. Then if something I say seems useful to you, make use of it to persuade us of your position."

I surely do wish that, said Cebes.

Listen then, and I will, Cebes, he said. When I was a young man I was wonderfully keen on that wisdom which they call natural science, for I thought it splendid to know the causes of everything, why it comes to be, why it perishes, and why it exists. I was often changing my mind in the investigation, in the first instance, of questions such as these: Are living creatures nurtured when heat and cold produce a kind of putrefaction, as some say? Do we think with our blood, or air, or fire, or none of these, and does the brain provide our senses of hearing and sight and smell, from which come memory and opinion, and from memory and opinion which has become stable, comes knowledge? Then again, as I investigated how these things perish and what happens to things in the sky and on the earth, finally I became convinced that I have no natural aptitude at all for that kind of investigation, and of this I will give you sufficient proof. This investigation made me quite blind even to those things which I and others thought that I clearly knew before, so that I unlearned what I thought I knew before, about many other things and specifically about how men grew. I thought before that it was obvious to anybody that men grew through eating and drinking, for food adds flesh to flesh and bones to bones, and in the same way appropriate parts were added to all other parts of the body, so that the man grew from an earlier small bulk to a large bulk later, and so a small man became big. That is what I thought then. Do you not think it was reasonable?

I do, said Cebes.

Then further consider this: I thought my opinion was satisfactory, that when a large man stood by a small one he was taller by a head, and so a horse was taller than a horse. Even clearer than this, I thought that ten was more than eight because two had been added, and that a

two-cubit length is larger than a cubit because it surpasses it by half
its length.

And what do you think now about those things?

That I am far, by Zeus, from believing that I know the cause of any
of those things. I will not even allow myself to say that where one is
added to one either the one to which it is added or the one that is
added becomes two, or that the one added and the one to which it   97
is added become two because of the addition of the one to the other.
I wonder that, when each of them is separate from the other, each of
them is one, nor are they then two, but that, when they come near to
one another, this is the cause of their becoming two, the coming
together and being placed closer to one another. Nor can I any longer
be persuaded that when one thing is divided, this division is the cause
of its becoming two, for just now the cause of becoming two was the   b
opposite. At that time it was their coming close together and one was
added to the other, but now it is because one is taken and separated
from the other.

I do not any longer persuade myself that I know why a unit or
anything else comes to be, or perishes or exists by the old method of
investigation, and I do not accept it, but I have a confused method of
my own. One day I heard someone reading, as he said, from a book   c
of Anaxagoras, and saying that it is Mind that directs and is the cause
of everything. I was delighted with this cause and it seemed to me good,
in a way, that Mind should be the cause of all. I thought that if this
were so, the directing Mind would direct everything and arrange each
thing in the way that was best. If then one wished to know the cause
of each thing, why it comes to be or perishes or exists, one had to find
what was the best way for it to be, or to be acted upon, or to act. On   d
these premises then it befitted a man to investigate only, about this and
other things, what is best. The same man must inevitably also know
what is worse, for that is part of the same knowledge. As I reflected on
this subject I was glad to think that I had found in Anaxagoras a teacher
about the cause of things after my own heart, and that he would tell   e
me, first, whether the earth is flat or round, and then would explain
why it is so of necessity, saying which is better, and that it was better
to be so. If he said it was in the middle of the universe, he would go
on to show that it was better for it to be in the middle, and if he showed
me those things I should be prepared never to desire any other kind   98
of cause. I was ready to find out in the same way about the sun and
the moon and the other heavenly bodies, about their relative speed,
their turnings, and whatever else happened to them, how it is best that

each should act or be acted upon. I never thought that Anaxagoras, who said that those things were directed by Mind, would bring in any other cause for them than that it was best for them to be as they are.

b Once he had given the best for each as the cause for each and the general cause of all, I thought he would go on to explain the common good for all, and I would not have exchanged my hopes for a fortune. I eagerly acquired his books and read them as quickly as I could in order to know the best and the worst as soon as possible.

This wonderful hope was dashed as I went on reading and saw that the man made no use of Mind, nor gave it any responsibility for the

c management of things, but mentioned as causes air and ether and water and many other strange things. That seemed to me much like saying that Socrates' actions are all due to his mind, and then in trying to tell the causes of everything I do, to say that the reason that I am sitting here is because my body consists of bones and sinews, because the bones are hard and are separated by joints, that the sinews are such as to contract and relax, that they surround the bones along with flesh

d and skin which hold them together, then as the bones are hanging in their sockets, the relaxation and contraction of the sinews enable me to bend my limbs, and that is the cause of my sitting here with my limbs bent.

Again, he would mention other such causes for my talking to you: sounds and air and hearing, and a thousand other such things, but he would neglect to mention the true causes, that, after the Athenians

e decided it was better to condemn me, for this reason it seemed best to me to sit here and more right to remain and to endure whatever penalty they ordered. For, by the dog, I think these sinews and bones could

99 long ago have been in Megara or among the Boeotians, taken there by my belief as to the best course, if I had not thought it more right and honorable to endure whatever penalty the city ordered rather than escape and run away. To call those things causes is too absurd. If someone said that without bones and sinews and all such things, I should not be able to do what I decided, he would be right, but surely to say that they are the cause of what I do, and not that I have chosen

b the best course, even though I act with my mind, is to speak very lazily and carelessly. Imagine not being able to distinguish the real cause from that without which the cause would not be able to act as a cause. It is what the majority appear to do, like people groping in the dark; they call it a cause, thus giving it a name that does not belong to it. That is why one man surrounds the earth with a vortex to make the

c heavens keep it in place, another makes the air support it like a wide

lid. As for their capacity of being in the best place they could possibly be put, this they do not look for, nor do they believe it to have any divine force, but they believe that they will some time discover a stronger and more immortal Atlas to hold everything together more, and they do not believe that the truly good and "binding" binds and holds them together. I would gladly become the disciple of any man who taught the workings of that kind of cause. However, since I was deprived and could neither discover it myself nor learn it from another, do you wish   d
me to give you an explanation of how, as a second best, I busied myself with the search for the cause, Cebes?

I would wish it above all else, he said.

After this, he said, when I had wearied of investigating things, I thought that I must be careful to avoid the experience of those who watch an eclipse of the sun, for some of them ruin their eyes unless they watch its reflection in water or some such material. A similar   e
thought crossed my mind, and I feared that my soul would be altogether blinded if I looked at things with my eyes and tried to grasp them with each of my senses. So I thought I must take refuge in discussions and investigate the truth of things by means of words. However, perhaps this analogy is inadequate, for I certainly do not admit that one who   100
investigates things by means of words is dealing with images any more than one who looks at facts. However, I started in this manner: taking as my hypothesis in each case the theory that seemed to me the most compelling, I would consider as true, about cause and everything else, whatever agreed with this, and as untrue whatever did not so agree. But I want to put my meaning more clearly, for I do not think that you understand me now.

No, by Zeus, said Cebes, not very well.

This, he said, is what I mean. It is nothing new, but what I have   b
never stopped talking about, both elsewhere and in the earlier part of our conversation. I am going to try to show you the kind of cause with which I have concerned myself. I turn back to those oft-mentioned things and proceed from them. I assume the existence of a Beautiful, itself by itself, of a Good and a Great and all the rest. If you grant me these and agree that they exist, I hope to show you the cause as a result, and to find the soul to be immortal.

Take it that I grant you this, said Cebes, and hasten to your con-   c
clusion.

Consider then, he said, whether you share my opinion as to what follows, for I think that, if there is anything beautiful besides the Beautiful itself, it is beautiful for no other reason than that it shares in that

Beautiful, and I say so with everything. Do you agree to this sort of cause? — I do.

d   I no longer understand or recognize those other sophisticated causes, and if someone tells me that a thing is beautiful because it has a bright color or shape or any such thing, I ignore these other reasons—for all these confuse me—but I simply, naively, and perhaps foolishly cling to this, that nothing else makes it beautiful other than the presence of, or the sharing in, or however you may describe its relationship to that Beautiful we mentioned, for I will not insist on the precise nature of the relationship, but that all beautiful things are beautiful by the Beauti-

e   ful. That, I think, is the safest answer I can give myself or anyone else. And if I stick to this I think I shall never fall into error. This is the safe answer for me or anyone else to give, namely, that it is through Beauty that beautiful things are made beautiful. Or do you not think so too? — I do.

And that it is through Bigness that big things are big and the bigger are bigger, and that smaller things are made small by Smallness? — Yes.

And you would not accept the statement that one man is taller than

101   another by a head and the shorter man shorter by the same, but you would bear witness that you mean nothing else than that everything that is bigger is made bigger by nothing else than by Bigness, and that is the cause of its being bigger, and the smaller is made smaller only by Smallness, and this is why it is smaller. I think you would be afraid that some opposite argument would confront you if you said that someone is bigger or smaller by a head, first, because the bigger is bigger and the smaller smaller by the same, then because the bigger is bigger by a

b   head which is small, and this would be strange, namely, that someone is made bigger by something small. Would you not be afraid of this?

I certainly would, said Cebes, laughing.

Then you would be afraid to say that ten is more numerous than eight by two, and that this is the cause of the excess, and not Numerousness and because of Numerousness, or that two cubits is bigger than one cubit by half and not by Bigness, for this is the same fear. — Certainly.

Then would you not avoid saying that when one is added to one it

c   is the addition and when it is divided it is the division that is the cause of two? And you would loudly exclaim that you do not know how else each thing can come to be except by sharing in the particular reality in which it shares, and in these cases you do not know of any other cause of becoming two except by sharing in Twoness, and that the things that are to be two must share in this, as that which is to be one

must share in Oneness, and you would dismiss these additions and divisions and other such subtleties, and leave them to those wiser than yourself to answer. But you, afraid, as they say, of your own shadow   d
and your inexperience, would cling to the safety of your own hypothesis and give that answer. If someone then attacked your hypothesis itself, you would ignore him and would not answer until you had examined whether the consequences that follow from it agree with one another or contradict one another.[14] And when you must give an account of your hypothesis itself you will proceed in the same way: you will assume another hypothesis, the one which seems to you best of the higher ones until you come to something acceptable, but you will not jumble the   e
two as the debaters do by discussing the hypothesis and its consequences at the same time, if you wish to discover any truth. This they do not discuss at all nor give any thought to, but their wisdom enables them to mix everything up and yet to be pleased with themselves, but if you   102
are a philosopher I think you will do as I say.

What you say is very true, said Simmias and Cebes together.

ECHECRATES: Yes, by Zeus, Phaedo, and they were right; I think he made these things wonderfully clear to anyone of even small intelligence.

PHAEDO: Yes indeed, Echecrates, and all those present thought so too.

ECHECRATES: And so do we who were not present but hear of it now. What was said after that?

PHAEDO: As I recall it, when the above had been accepted, and it was agreed that each of the Forms existed, and that other things acquired   b
their name by having a share in them, he followed this up by asking: If you say these things are so, when you then say that Simmias is taller than Socrates but shorter than Phaedo, do you not mean that there is in Simmias both tallness and shortness? — I do.

But, he said, do you agree that the words of the statement "Simmias is taller than Socrates" do not express the truth of the matter? It is not,   c
surely, the nature of Simmias to be taller than Socrates because he is Simmias but because of the tallness he happens to have? Nor is he taller than Socrates because Socrates is Socrates, but because Socrates has smallness compared with the tallness of the other? — True.

---

14. Alternatively: "If someone should cling to your hypothesis itself, you would dismiss him and would not answer until you had examined whether the consequences that follow from it agree with one another or contradict one another."

Nor is he shorter than Phaedo because Phaedo is Phaedo, but because Phaedo has tallness compared with the shortness of Simmias? — That is so.

d   So then Simmias is called both short and tall, being between the two, presenting his shortness to be overcome by the tallness of one, and his tallness to overcome the shortness of the other. He smilingly added, I seem to be going to talk like a book, but it is as I say. The other agreed.

My purpose is that you may agree with me. Now it seems to me that not only Tallness itself is never willing to be tall and short at the same time, but also that the tallness in us will never admit the short

e   or be overcome, but one of two things happens: either it flees and retreats whenever its opposite, the short, approaches, or it is destroyed by its approach. It is not willing to endure and admit shortness and be other than it was, whereas I admit and endure shortness and still remain the same person and am this short man. But Tallness, being tall, cannot venture to be small. In the same way, the short in us is unwilling to become or to be tall ever, nor does any other of the opposites become

103 or be its opposite while still being what it was; either it goes away or is destroyed when that happens. — I altogether agree, said Cebes.

When he heard this, someone of those present—I have no clear memory of who it was—said: "By the gods, did we not agree earlier in our discussion[15] to the very opposite of what is now being said, namely, that the larger came from the smaller and the smaller from the larger, and that this simply was how opposites came to be, from their opposites, but now I think we are saying that this would never happen?"

On hearing this, Socrates inclined his head towards the speaker and said: "You have bravely reminded us, but you do not understand the

b   difference between what is said now and what was said then, which was that an opposite thing came from an opposite thing; now we say that the opposite itself could never become opposite to itself, neither that in us nor that in nature. Then, my friend, we were talking of things that have opposite qualities and naming these after them, but now we say that these opposites themselves, from the presence of which in them things get their name, never can tolerate the coming to be from one

c   another." At the same time he looked to Cebes and said: "Does anything of what this man says also disturb you?"

---

15. The reference is to 70d–71a above.

Not at the moment, said Cebes, but I do not deny that many things do disturb me.

We are altogether agreed then, he said, that an opposite will never be opposite to itself. — Entirely agreed.

Consider then whether you will agree to this further point. There is something you call hot and something you call cold. — There is.

Are they the same as what you call snow and fire? — By Zeus, no.   d

So the hot is something other than fire, and the cold is something other than snow? — Yes.

You think, I believe, that being snow it will not admit the hot, as we said before, and remain what it was and be both snow and hot, but when the hot approaches it will either retreat before it or be destroyed. — Quite so.

So fire, as the cold approaches, will either go away or be destroyed; it will never venture to admit coldness and remain what it was, fire and cold. — What you say is true.   e

It is true then about some of these things that not only the Form itself deserves its own name for all time, but there is something else that is not the Form but has its character whenever it exists. Perhaps I can make my meaning clearer: the Odd must always be given this name we now mention. Is that not so? — Certainly.

Is it the only one of existing things to be called odd—this is my question—or is there something else than the Odd which one must   104 nevertheless also always call odd, as well as by its own name, because it is such by nature as never to be separated from the Odd? I mean, for example, the number three and many others. Consider three: do you not think that it must always be called both by its own name and by that of the Odd, which is not the same as three? That is the nature of three, and of five, and of half of all the numbers; each of them is odd, but it is not the Odd. Then again, two and four and the whole   b other column of numbers; each of them, while not being the same as the Even, is always even. Do you not agree? — Of course.

Look now. What I want to make clear is this: Not only do those opposites not admit each other, but this is also true of those things which, while not being opposite to each other yet always contain the opposites, and it seems that these do not admit that Form which is opposite to that which is in them; when it approaches them, they either perish or give way. Shall we not say that three will perish or undergo   c anything before, while remaining three, becoming even? — Certainly, said Cebes.

Yet surely two is not the opposite of three? — Indeed it is not.

It is then not only opposite Forms that do not admit each other's approach, but also some other things that do not admit the onset of opposites. — Very true.

Do you then want us, if we can, to define what these are? — I surely do.

d Would they be the things that compel whatever they occupy not only to contain their Form but also always that of some opposite? — How do you mean?

As we were saying just now, you surely know that what the Form of three occupies must be not only three but also odd. — Certainly.

And we say that the opposite Form to the Form that achieves this result could never come to it. — It could not.

Now it is Oddness that has done this? — Yes.

And opposite to this is the Form of the Even? — Yes.

e So then the Form of the Even will never come to three? — Never.

Then three has no share in the Even? — Never.

So three is uneven? — Yes.

As for what I said we must define, that is, what kind of things, while not being opposites to something, yet do not admit the opposite, as, for example, the triad, though it is not the opposite of the Even, yet does

105 not admit it because it always brings along the opposite of the Even, and so the dyad in relation to the Odd, fire to the Cold, and very many other things, see whether you would define it thus: Not only does the opposite not admit its opposite, but that which brings along some opposite into that which it occupies; that which brings this along will not admit the opposite to that which it brings along. Refresh your memory; it is no worse for being heard often. Five does not admit the form of the Even, nor will ten, its double, admit the form of the Odd. The double itself is an opposite of something else, yet it will not admit

b the form of the Odd. Nor do one-and-a-half and other such fractions admit the form of the Whole, nor will one-third, and so on, if you follow me and agree to this.

I certainly agree, he said, and I follow you.

Tell me again from the beginning, he said, and do not answer in the words of the question, but do as I do. I say that beyond that safe answer, which I spoke of first, I see another safe answer. If you should

c ask me what, coming into a body, makes it hot, my reply would not be that safe and ignorant one, that it is heat, but our present argument provides a more sophisticated answer, namely, fire, and if you ask me what, on coming into a body, makes it sick, I will not say sickness but fever. Nor, if asked the presence of what in a number makes it odd, I will not say oddness but oneness, and so with other things. See if you now sufficiently understand what I want. — Quite sufficiently.

Answer me then, he said, what is it that, present in a body, makes it living? — A soul.

And is that always so? — Of course.   d

Whatever the soul occupies, it always brings life to it? — It does.

Is there, or is there not, an opposite to life? — There is.

What is it? — Death.

So the soul will never admit the opposite of that which it brings along, as we agree from what has been said?

Most certainly, said Cebes.

Well, and what do we call that which does not admit the form of the even? — The uneven.

What do we call that which will not admit the just and that which will not admit the musical?

The unmusical, and the other the unjust.   e

Very well, what do we call that which does not admit death?

The deathless, he said.

Now the soul does not admit death? — No.

So the soul is deathless? — It is.

Very well, he said. Shall we say that this has been proved, do you think?

Quite adequately proved, Socrates.

Well now, Cebes, he said, if the uneven were of necessity indestructible, surely three would be indestructible? — Of course.   106

And if the non-hot were of necessity indestructible, then whenever anyone brought heat to snow, the snow would retreat safe and unthawed, for it could not be destroyed, nor again could it stand its ground and admit the heat? — What you say is true.

In the same way, if the non-cold were indestructible, then when some cold attacked the fire, it would neither be quenched nor destroyed, but retreat safely. — Necessarily.

Must then the same not be said of the deathless? If the deathless is   b
also indestructible, it is impossible for the soul to be destroyed when death comes upon it. For it follows from what has been said that it will not admit death or be dead, just as three, we said, will not be even nor will the odd; nor will fire be cold, nor the heat that is in the fire. But, someone might say, what prevents the odd, while not becoming even   c

as has been agreed, from being destroyed, and the even to come to be instead? We could not maintain against the man who said this that it is not destroyed, for the uneven is not indestructible. If we had agreed that it was indestructible, we could easily have maintained that at the coming of the even, the odd and the three have gone away and the same would hold for fire and the hot and the other things. — Surely.

d   And so now, if we are agreed that the deathless is indestructible, the soul, besides being deathless, is indestructible. If not, we need another argument.

There is no need for one as far as that goes, for hardly anything could resist destruction if the deathless, which lasts forever, would admit destruction.

All would agree, said Socrates, that the god, and the Form of life itself, and anything that is deathless, are never destroyed. — All men would agree, by Zeus, to that, and the gods, I imagine, even more so.

e   If the deathless is indestructible, then the soul, if it is deathless, would also be indestructible? — Necessarily.

Then when death comes to man, the mortal part of him dies, it seems, but his deathless part goes away safe and indestructible, yielding the place to death. — So it appears.

107   Therefore the soul, Cebes, he said, is most certainly deathless and indestructible and our souls will really dwell in the underworld.

I have nothing more to say against that, Socrates, said Cebes, nor can I doubt your arguments. If Simmias here or someone else has something to say, he should not remain silent, for I do not know to what further occasion other than the present he could put it off if he wants to say or to hear anything on these subjects.

Certainly, said Simmias, I myself have no remaining grounds for doubt after what has been said; nevertheless, in view of the importance

b   of our subject and my low opinion of human weakness, I am bound still to have some private misgivings about what we have said.

You are not only right to say this, Simmias, Socrates said, but our first hypotheses require clearer examination, even though we find them convincing. And if you analyze them adequately, you will, I think, follow the argument as far as a man can, and if the conclusion is clear, you will look no further. — That is true.

c   It is right to think then, gentlemen, that if the soul is immortal, it requires our care not only for the time we call our life, but for the sake of all time, and that one is in terrible danger if one does not give it that care. If death were escape from everything, it would be a great boon to the wicked to get rid of the body and of their wickedness together with their soul. But now that the soul appears to be immortal, there is no escape from evil or salvation for it except by becoming as good and wise as possible, for the soul goes to the underworld possessing nothing but its education and upbringing, which are said to bring the greatest benefit or harm to the dead right at the beginning of the journey yonder.

We are told that when each person dies, the guardian spirit who was allotted to him in life proceeds to lead him to a certain place, whence those who have been gathered together there must, after being judged, proceed to the underworld with the guide who has been appointed to lead them thither from here. Having there undergone what they must and stayed there the appointed time, they are led back here by another guide after long periods of time. The journey is not as Aeschylus' Telephus[16] describes it. He says that only one single path leads to Hades, but I think it is neither one nor simple, for then there would be no need of guides; one could not make any mistake if there were but one path. As it is, it is likely to have many forks and crossroads; and I base this judgment on the sacred rites and customs here.

The well-ordered and wise soul follows the guide and is not without familiarity with its surroundings, but the soul that is passionately attached to the body, as I said before, hovers around it and the visible world for a long time, struggling and suffering much until it is led away by force and with difficulty by its appointed spirit. When the impure soul which has performed some impure deed joins the others after being involved in unjust killings, or committed other crimes which are akin to these and are actions of souls of this kind, everybody shuns it and turns away, unwilling to be its fellow traveler or its guide; such a soul wanders alone completely at a loss until a certain time arrives and it is forcibly led to its proper dwelling place. On the other hand, the soul that has led a pure and moderate life finds fellow travelers and gods to guide it, and each of them dwells in a place suited to it.

There are many strange places upon the earth, and the earth itself is not such as those who are used to discourse upon it believe it to be in nature or size, as someone has convinced me.

Simmias said: "What do you mean, Socrates? I have myself heard many things said about the earth, but certainly not the things that convince you. I should be glad to hear them."

---

16. The *Telephus* of Aeschylus is not extant.

Indeed, Simmias, I do not think it requires the skill of Glaucus[17] to tell you what they are, but to prove them true requires more than that skill, and I should perhaps not be able to do so. Also, even if I had the knowledge, my remaining time would not be long enough to tell the tale. However, nothing prevents my telling you what I am convinced is the shape of the earth and what its regions are.

Even that is sufficient, said Simmias.

Well then, he said, the first thing of which I am convinced is that if the earth is a sphere in the middle of the heavens, it has no need of air or any other force to prevent it from falling. The homogeneous nature of the heavens on all sides and the earth's own equipoise are sufficient to hold it, for an object balanced in the middle of something homogeneous will have no tendency to incline more in any direction than any other but will remain unmoved. This, he said, is the first point of which I am persuaded.

And rightly so, said Simmias.

Further, the earth is very large, and we live around the sea in a small portion of it between Phasis and the pillars of Heracles, like ants or frogs around a swamp; many other peoples live in many such parts of it. Everywhere about the earth there are numerous hollows of many kinds and shapes and sizes into which the water and the mist and the air have gathered. The earth itself is pure and lies in the pure sky where the stars are situated, which the majority of those who discourse on these subjects call the ether. The water and mist and air are the sediment of the ether and they always flow into the hollows of the earth. We, who dwell in the hollows of it, are unaware of this and we think that we live above, on the surface of the earth. It is as if someone who lived deep down in the middle of the ocean thought he was living on its surface. Seeing the sun and the other heavenly bodies through the water, he would think the sea to be the sky; because he is slow and weak, he has never reached the surface of the sea or risen with his head above the water or come out of the sea to our region here, nor seen how much purer and more beautiful it is than his own region, nor has he ever heard of it from anyone who has seen it.

Our experience is the same: Living in a certain hollow of the earth, we believe that we live upon its surface; the air we call the heavens, as if the stars made their way through it; this too is the same: Because

17. A proverbial expression whose origin, and whose specific meaning, is obscure.

of our weakness and slowness we are not able to make our way to the   e
upper limit of the air; if anyone got to this upper limit, if anyone came
to it or reached it on wings and his head rose above it, then just as fish
on rising from the sea see things in our region, he would see things
there and, if his nature could endure to contemplate them, he would
know that there is the true heaven, the true light, and the true earth,
for the earth here, these stones and the whole region, are spoiled and   110
eaten away, just as things in the sea are by the salt water.

Nothing worth mentioning grows in the sea, nothing, one might
say, is fully developed; there are caves and sand and endless slime and
mud wherever there is earth—not comparable in any way with the
beauties of our region. So those things above are in their turn far
superior to the things we know. Indeed, if this is the moment to tell a
tale, Simmias, it is worth hearing about the nature of things on the   b
surface of the earth under the heavens.

At any rate, Socrates, said Simmias, we should be glad to hear
this story.

Well then, my friend, in the first place it is said that the earth, looked
at from above, looks like those spherical balls made up of twelve pieces
of leather; it is multicolored, and of these colors those used by our
painters give us an indication; up there the whole earth has these colors,   c
but much brighter and purer than these; one part is sea-green and of
marvelous beauty, another is golden, another is white, whiter than chalk
or snow; the earth is composed also of the other colors, more numerous
and beautiful than any we have seen. The very hollows of the earth,
full of water and air, gleaming among the variety of other colors, present   d
a color of their own so that the whole is seen as a continuum of
variegated colors. On the surface of the earth the plants grow with
corresponding beauty, the trees and the flowers and the fruits, and so
with the hills and the stones, more beautiful in their smoothness and
transparency and color. Our precious stones here are but fragments,
our cornelians, jaspers, emeralds, and the rest. All stones there are of   e
that kind, and even more beautiful. The reason is that there they are
pure, not eaten away or spoiled by decay and brine, or corroded by the
water and air which have flowed into the hollows here and bring ugliness
and disease upon earth, stones, the other animals, and plants. The earth
itself is adorned with all these things, and also with gold and silver   111
and other metals. These stand out, being numerous and massive and
occurring everywhere, so that the earth is a sight for the blessed. There
are many other living creatures upon the earth, and also men, some

living inland, others at the edge of the air, as we live on the edge of the sea, others again live on islands surrounded by air close to the b mainland. In a word, what water and the sea are to us, the air is to them, and the ether is to them what the air is to us. The climate is such that they are without disease, and they live much longer than people do here; their eyesight, hearing, and intelligence and all such are as superior to ours as air is superior to water and ether to air in purity; they have groves and temples dedicated to the gods, in which the gods really dwell, and they communicate with them by speech and c prophecy and by the sight of them; they see the sun and moon and stars as they are, and in other ways their happiness is in accord with this.

This then is the nature of the earth as a whole and of its surroundings; around the whole of it there are many regions in the hollows; some are deeper and more open than that in which we live; others are deeper d and have a narrower opening than ours, and there are some that have less depth and more width. All these are connected with each other below the surface of the earth in many places by narrow and broader channels, and thus have outlets through which much water flows from one to another as into mixing bowls; huge rivers of both hot and cold water thus flow beneath the earth eternally, much fire and large rivers e of fire, and many of wet mud, both more pure and more muddy, such as those flowing in advance of the lava and the stream of lava itself in Sicily. These streams then fill up every and all regions as the flow reaches each, and all these places move up and down with the oscillating movement of the earth. The natural cause of the oscillation is as follows:
112 One of the hollows of the earth, which is also the biggest, pierces through the whole earth; it is that which Homer mentioned when he said: "Far down where is the deepest pit below the earth . . . ,"[18] and which he elsewhere, and many other poets, call Tartarus; into this chasm all the rivers flow together, and again flow out of it, and each b river is affected by the nature of the land through which it flows. The reason for their flowing into and out of Tartarus is that this water has no bottom or solid base but it oscillates up and down in waves, and the air and wind about it do the same, for they follow it when it flows to this or that part of the earth. Just as when people breathe, the flow of air goes in and out, so here the air oscillates with the water and c creates terrible winds as it goes in and out. Whenever the water retreats to what we call the lower part of the earth, it flows into those parts and

---

18. *Iliad* viii.14; cf. viii.481.

fills them up as if the water were pumped in; when it leaves that part
for this, it fills these parts again, and the parts filled flow through the
channels and through the earth and in each case arrive at the places
to which the channels lead and create seas and marshes and rivers and
springs. From there the waters flow under the earth again, some flowing   d
around larger and more numerous regions, some around smaller and
shallower ones, then flow back into Tartarus, some at a point much
lower than where they issued forth, others only a little way, but all of
them at a lower point, some of them at the opposite side of the chasm,
some on the same side; some flow in a wide circle round the earth
once or many times like snakes, then go as far down as possible, then
go back into the chasm of Tartarus. From each side it is possible to   e
flow down as far as the center, but not beyond, for this part that faces
the river flow from either side is steep.

There are many other large rivers of all kinds, and among these
there are four of note; the biggest which flows on the outside (of the
earth) in a circle is called Oceanus; opposite it and flowing in the
opposite direction is the Acheron; it flows through many other deserted   113
regions and further underground makes its way to the Acherusian lake
to which the souls of the majority come after death and, after remaining
there for a certain appointed time, longer for some, shorter for others,
they are sent back to birth as living creatures. The third river issues
between the first two, and close to its source it falls into a region burning
with much fire and makes a lake larger than our sea, boiling with water
and mud. From there it goes in a circle, foul and muddy, and winding   b
on its way it comes, among other places, to the edge of the Acherusian
lake but does not mingle with its waters; then, coiling many times
underground it flows lower down into Tartarus; this is called the Pyriphlegethon, and its lava streams throw off fragments of it in various
parts of the earth. Opposite this the fourth river issues forth, which is
called Stygion, and it is said to flow first into a terrible and wild region,   c
all of it blue-gray in color, and the lake that this river forms by flowing
into it is called the Styx. As its waters fall into the lake they acquire
dread powers; then diving below and winding round it flows in the
opposite direction from the Pyriphlegethon and into the opposite side
of the Acherusian lake; its waters do not mingle with any other; it too
flows in a circle and into Tartarus opposite the Pyriphlegethon. The
name of that fourth river, the poets tell us, is Cocytus.[19]

---

19. For these features of the underworld, see *Odyssey* x.511 ff., xi.157.

d   Such is the nature of these things. When the dead arrive at the place to which each has been led by his guardian spirit, they are first judged as to whether they have led a good and pious life. Those who have lived an average life make their way to the Acheron and embark upon such vessels as there are for them and proceed to the lake. There they

e dwell and are purified by penalties for any wrongdoing they may have committed; they are also suitably rewarded for their good deeds as each deserves. Those who are deemed incurable because of the enormity of their crimes, having committed many great sacrileges or wicked and unlawful murders and other such wrongs—their fitting fate is to be hurled into Tartarus never to emerge from it. Those who are deemed to have committed great but curable crimes, such as doing violence to

114 their father or mother in a fit of temper but who have felt remorse for the rest of their lives, or who have killed someone in a similar manner, these must of necessity be thrown into Tartarus, but a year later the current throws them out, those who are guilty of murder by way of Cocytus, and those who have done violence to their parents by way of the Pyriphlegethon. After they have been carried along to the Acheru-sian lake, they cry out and shout, some for those they have killed, others for those they have maltreated, and calling them they then pray to them

b and beg them to allow them to step out into the lake and to receive them. If they persuade them, they do step out and their punishment comes to an end; if they do not, they are taken back into Tartarus and from there into the rivers, and this does not stop until they have per-suaded those they have wronged, for this is the punishment which the judges imposed on them.

c   Those who are deemed to have lived an extremely pious life are freed and released from the regions of the earth as from a prison; they make their way up to a pure dwelling place and live on the surface of the earth. Those who have purified themselves sufficiently by philoso-phy live in the future altogether without a body; they make their way to even more beautiful dwelling places which it is hard to describe clearly, nor do we now have the time to do so. Because of the things we have enunciated, Simmias, one must make every effort to share in virtue and wisdom in one's life, for the reward is beautiful and the hope is great.

d   No sensible man would insist that these things are as I have described them, but I think it is fitting for a man to risk the belief—for the risk is a noble one—that this, or something like this, is true about our souls and their dwelling places, since the soul is evidently immortal, and a man should repeat this to himself as if it were an incantation, which is why I have been prolonging my tale. That is the reason why a man should be of good cheer about his own soul, if during life he has ignored the pleasures of the body and its ornamentation as of no concern to him and doing him more harm than good, but has seriously concerned himself with the pleasures of learning, and adorned his soul not with alien but with its own ornaments, namely, moderation, righteousness, courage, freedom, and truth, and in that state awaits his journey to the underworld.

Now you, Simmias, Cebes, and the rest of you, Socrates continued, will each take that journey at some other time but my fated day calls me now, as a tragic character might say, and it is about time for me to have my bath, for I think it better to have it before I drink the poison and save the women the trouble of washing the corpse.

When Socrates had said this Crito spoke. Very well, Socrates, what are your instructions to me and the others about your children or anything else? What can we do that would please you most? — Nothing new, Crito, said Socrates, but what I am always saying, that you will please me and mine and yourselves by taking good care of your own selves in whatever you do, even if you do not agree with me now, but if you neglect your own selves, and are unwilling to live following the tracks, as it were, of what we have said now and on previous occasions, you will achieve nothing even if you strongly agree with me at this moment.

We shall be eager to follow your advice, said Crito, but how shall we bury you?

In any way you like, said Socrates, if you can catch me and I do not escape you. And laughing quietly, looking at us, he said: I do not convince Crito that I am this Socrates talking to you here and ordering all I say, but he thinks that I am the thing which he will soon be looking at as a corpse, and so he asks how he shall bury me. I have been saying for some time and at some length that after I have drunk the poison I shall no longer be with you but will leave you to go and enjoy some good fortunes of the blessed, but it seems that I have said all this to him in vain in an attempt to reassure you and myself too. Give a pledge to Crito on my behalf, he said, the opposite pledge to that he gave the jury. He pledged that I would stay; you must pledge that I will not stay after I die, but that I shall go away, so that Crito will bear it more easily when he sees my body being burned or buried and will not be angry on my behalf, as if I were suffering terribly, and so that he should not say at the funeral that he is laying out, or carrying out, or burying Socrates. For know you well, my dear Crito, that to express oneself badly is not only faulty as far as the language goes, but does some harm to the soul. You must be of good cheer, and say you are burying my body, and bury it in any way you like and think most customary.

After saying this he got up and went to another room to take his bath, and Crito followed him and he told us to wait for him. So we stayed, talking among ourselves, questioning what had been said, and then again talking of the great misfortune that had befallen us. We all felt as if we had lost a father and would be orphaned for the rest of our lives. When he had washed, his children were brought to him—two of his sons were small and one was older—and the women of his household came to him. He spoke to them before Crito and gave them what instructions he wanted. Then he sent the women and children away, and he himself joined us. It was now close to sunset, for he had stayed inside for some time. He came and sat down after his bath and conversed for a short while, when the officer of the Eleven came and stood by him and said: "I shall not reproach you as I do the others, Socrates. They are angry with me and curse me when, obeying the orders of my superiors, I tell them to drink the poison. During the time you have been here I have come to know you in other ways as the noblest, the gentlest, and the best man who has ever come here. So now too I know that you will not make trouble for me; you know who is responsible and you will direct your anger against them. You know what message I bring. Fare you well, and try to endure what you must as easily as possible." The officer was weeping as he turned away and went out. Socrates looked up at him and said: "Fare you well also; we shall do as you bid us." And turning to us he said: "How pleasant the man is! During the whole time I have been here he has come in and conversed with me from time to time, a most agreeable man. And how genuinely he now weeps for me. Come, Crito, let us obey him. Let someone bring the poison if it is ready; if not, let the man prepare it."

But Socrates, said Crito, I think the sun still shines upon the hills and has not yet set. I know that others drink the poison quite a long time after they have received the order, eating and drinking quite a bit, and some of them enjoy intimacy with their loved ones. Do not hurry; there is still some time.

It is natural, Crito, for them to do so, said Socrates, for they think they derive some benefit from doing this, but it is not fitting for me. I do not expect any benefit from drinking the poison a little later, except to become ridiculous in my own eyes for clinging to life, and be sparing of it when there is none left. So do as I ask and do not refuse me.

Hearing this, Crito nodded to the slave who was standing near him; the slave went out and after a time came back with the man who was to administer the poison, carrying it made ready in a cup. When Socrates saw him he said: "Well, my good man, you are an expert in this; what must one do?" — "Just drink it and walk around until your legs feel heavy, and then lie down and it will act of itself." And he offered the b cup to Socrates, who took it quite cheerfully, Echecrates, without a tremor or any change of feature or color, but looking at the man from under his eyebrows as was his wont, asked: "What do you say about pouring a libation from this drink? It is allowed?" — "We only mix as much as we believe will suffice," said the man.

I understand, Socrates said, but one is allowed, indeed one must, c utter a prayer to the gods that the journey from here to yonder may be fortunate. This is my prayer and may it be so.

And while he was saying this, he was holding the cup, and then drained it calmly and easily. Most of us had been able to hold back our tears reasonably well up till then, but when we saw him drinking it and after he drank it, we could hold them back no longer; my own tears came in floods against my will. So I covered my face. I was weeping for myself, not for him—for my misfortune in being deprived of such d a comrade. Even before me, Crito was unable to restrain his tears and got up. Apollodorus had not ceased from weeping before, and at this moment his noisy tears and anger made everybody present break down, except Socrates. "What is this," he said, "you strange fellows. It is mainly for this reason that I sent the women away, to avoid such unseemliness, e for I am told one should die in good omened silence. So keep quiet and control yourselves."

His words made us ashamed, and we checked our tears. He walked around, and when he said his legs were heavy he lay on his back as he had been told to do, and the man who had given him the poison touched his body, and after a while tested his feet and legs, pressed hard upon his foot, and asked him if he felt this, and Socrates said no. 118 Then he pressed his calves, and made his way up his body and showed us that it was cold and stiff. He felt it himself and said that when the cold reached his heart he would be gone. As his belly was getting cold Socrates uncovered his head—he had covered it—and said—these were his last words — "Crito, we owe a cock to Asclepius;[20] make this offering

---

20. A cock was sacrificed to Asclepius by the sick people who slept in his temples, hoping for a cure. Socrates apparently means that death is a cure for the ills of life.

118a   to him and do not forget." — "It shall be done," said Crito, "tell us if there is anything else." But there was no answer. Shortly afterwards Socrates made a movement; the man uncovered him and his eyes were fixed. Seeing this Crito closed his mouth and his eyes.

    Such was the end of our comrade, Echecrates, a man who, we would say, was of all those we have known the best, and also the wisest and the most upright.

SUGGESTIONS FOR FURTHER READING

Socrates and Plato's Socratic Dialogues

1. Benson, Hugh H., ed. *Essays on the Philosophy of Socrates*, Oxford, 1992. Has extensive bibliography.
2. Kraut, Richard, ed. *The Cambridge Companion to Plato*, Cambridge, 1992. Comprehensive discussions of all aspects of Plato's work. Chapters 4, 5, and 6 are specially relevant to the dialogues printed here. Has extensive bibliography.
3. Nehamas, Alexander. *The Art of Living*, Berkeley, 1998.
4. Vlastos, Gregory, ed. *The Philosophy of Socrates: A Collection of Critical Essays*, New York, 1971.
5. ———. *Socrates: Ironist and Moral Philosopher*, Ithaca, N.Y., 1991.

Euthyphro

6. Cohen, S. Marc. "Socrates on the Definition of Piety: *Euthyphro* 10a–11b," *Journal of the History of Philosophy* 9 (1971), repr. in (4), 158–76.
7. Geach, Peter T. "Plato's *Euthyphro*: An Analysis and Commentary," *The Monist* 50 (1966):369–82.
8. Kidd, Ian. "The Case of Homicide in Plato's *Euthyphro*," in E. M. Craik, ed., *Owls to Athens*, Oxford, 1990, 213–22.
9. MacPherran, Mark. "Socratic Piety in the *Euthyphro*," *Journal of the History of Philosophy* 23 (1985), repr. in (1), 220–41.
10. Mann, William. "Piety: Lending Euthyphro a Hand," *Philosophy and Phenomenological Research* 58 (1998):123–42.
11. Taylor, Christopher C. W. "The End of the *Euthyphro*," *Phronesis* 27 (1982):109–18.

Apology

12. Brickhouse, Thomas C., and Nicholas D. Smith. *Socrates on Trial*, Oxford, 1989.
13. Burnyeat, Myles F. "The Impiety of Socrates," *Ancient Philosophy* 17 (1997):1–12.
14. Reeve, C. D. C. *Socrates in the Apology*, Indianapolis, 1989.
15. Stone, I. F. *The Trial of Socrates*, New York, 1988; with Myles F. Burnyeat, "Review of *The Trial of Socrates*, by I. F. Stone," *New York Review of Books* 35 (1988):12–18.

Crito

16. Bostock, David. "The Interpretation of Plato's *Crito*," *Phronesis* 35 (1990):1–20.
17. Kraut, Richard. *Socrates and the State*, Princeton, 1984.
18. Woozley, Anthony D. *Law and Obedience: The Arguments of Plato's Crito*, Chapel Hill, 1979.

Meno

19. Dimas, P. "True Belief in the *Meno*," *Oxford Studies in Ancient Philosophy* 14 (1996):1–32.
20. Irwin, T. H. *Plato's Ethics*, chap. 9, "Socratic Method and Socratic Ethics: The *Meno*," Oxford, 1995, 127–47.
21. Nehamas, Alexander. "*Meno*'s Paradox and Socrates as a Teacher," *Oxford Studies in Ancient Philosophy* 3 (1985):1–30. Reprinted in H. Benson, ed., *Essays on the Philosophy of Socrates*, New York, 1992, and in Nehamas, *Virtues of Authenticity*, Princeton, 1999.

Phaedo

22. Bostock, David. *Plato's Phaedo*, Oxford, 1986.
23. Frey, Roger G. "Did Socrates Commit Suicide?" *Philosophy* 53 (1978): 106–8.
24. Gallop, David. *Plato: Phaedo*, tr. with notes, Oxford, 1975.
25. Gill, Christopher. "The Death of Socrates," *Classical Quarterly* 23 (1973): 25–8.
26. Matthews, Gareth B., and Thomas Blackson. "Causes in the *Phaedo*," *Synthèse* 79 (1989):581–91.
27. Nehamas, Alexander. "Predication and Forms of Opposites in the *Phaedo*," *Review of Metaphysics* 26 (1973):461–91.
28. Scott, Dominic. "Platonic Recollection," in G. Fine, ed., *Plato 1: Metaphysics and Epistemology*, Oxford, 1999.
29. Vlastos, Gregory. "Reasons and Causes," *Philosophical Review* 78 (1969):291–325. Reprinted in Vlastos, *Platonic Studies*, 2nd ed., Princeton, 1981.